YESTERDAY'S STORIES

Recent Titles in
Contributions in American Studies

YESTERDAY'S STORIES

Popular Women's Novels
of the Twenties and Thirties

PATRICIA RAUB

Contributions in American Studies, Number 104
Robert H. Walker, Series Editor

GREENWOOD PRESS
Westport, Connecticut
London

Library of Congress Cataloging-in-Publication Data

Raub, Patricia.
   Yesterday's stories : popular women's novels of the twenties and
thirties / Patricia Raub.
      p. cm.—(Contributions in American studies, ISSN 0084–9227
; no. 104)
   Includes bibliographical references and index.
   ISBN 0–313–29259–0 (alk. paper)
   1. American fiction—Women authors—History and criticism.
2. Women—United States—Books and reading—History—20th century.
3. Women and literature—United States—History—20th century.
4. Popular literature—United States—History and criticism.
5. American fiction—20th century—History and criticism.
I. Title. II. Series.
PS674.W6R38 1994
813'.52099287—dc20   94–4794

British Library Cataloguing in Publication Data is available.

Library of Congress Catalog Card Number: 94–4794
ISBN: 0–313–29259–0
ISSN: 0084–9227

First published in 1994

Greenwood Press, 88 Post Road West, Westport, CT 06881
An imprint of Greenwood Publishing Group, Inc.

Printed in the United States of America

∞™

The paper used in this book complies with the
Permanent Paper Standard issued by the National
Information Standards Organization (Z39.48–1984).

10 9 8 7 6 5 4 3 2 1

This book is dedicated to my mother, Mildred Thomas Raub.

Contents

Acknowledgments

I thank Kathleen Vernon at the Knight Memorial Library for her help in locating long-forgotten best sellers, Barbara Farrell at Phillips Memorial Library at Providence College for her assistance with interlibrary loans, and Julia Tryon, also at Phillips Memorial Library, for her patience in directing me to the appropriate reference sources.

I am grateful to Robert Macieski, who read a rough draft of the first chapter, and to David Stineback, who read an equally rough draft of the last one. Both of them offered many useful suggestions. I am also thankful for the comments and reactions offered by the editors and readers at *American Studies*, who critiqued two successive drafts of the first chapter.

I appreciate the advice and encouragement I received from a number of supportive relatives, and I thank Doris Haisley, Iva Thomas, Linda and Paul Helvig, Millie and Joe Raub, and Susan Raub Rosen for their help and good will.

Most of all, I am indebted to my colleague and husband Robbie Goff, whose wide reading in cultural studies and insight into popular culture provided direction as this project inched toward completion. Rob generously set aside his own work to share in the conception, writing, and revision of this study. Without his guidance and his steadfast belief in my work, this book could not have been written.

Introduction

Popular taste is fleeting, as witnessed by contemporary reception of women's novels once in demand in America. Today, few have read, or even heard of, such best-selling novels of the 1920s and 1930s as Kathleen Norris's *Harriet and the Piper* (1920), Gertrude Atherton's *Black Oxen* (1923), Vina Delmar's *Bad Girl* (1928), Gladys Hasty Carroll's *As the Earth Turns* (1933), or Caroline Miller's *Lamb in His Bosom* (1933). Yet, tens of thousands once read these books, and public libraries stocked multiple copies of these novels in order to satisfy patron demand. Despite—or, perhaps, because of—the fact that few of these books continued to engage readers past the decade of their publication, popular novels written by women for a predominately female audience are of particular value to the cultural historian. "The time-bound nature of the best seller," Erik Lofroth observes in *A World Made Safe: Values and American Best Sellers, 1895–1920* (1983), "is of course precisely what makes it a suitable medium for an exploration of values that are current in a specific era." (15)

In this book I shall examine common attitudes and perceptions held by and about middle-class women in the Twenties and Thirties by analyzing the novels such women read most frequently. The interval between the two World Wars is a period of particular interest to those concerned with examining women's past perceptions and sensibility. During this time, middle-class women's lives were touched—and sometimes greatly altered—by a number of interconnecting changes in national social patterns which were precipitated by, and, in turn, precipitated, changes in women's values and attitudes. While few middle-class women of the day left a written record of the ways in which these trends impacted upon their own lives or of the degree to which their self-concept and their expectation of themselves as women were being transformed, we do know which books most appealed to them. We cannot, of course, assume that readers found themselves realistically depicted in these novels; it is unlikely that these novels can provide us with a literal transcription of the actual lives led by their readers. It is equally unlikely that writers and readers invariably spoke with one voice, that a given popular author expressed precisely the views and emotions of the majority of her readers. Nevertheless, by isolating patterns embedded in a number of successful works of the period, we can uncover values and attitudes widely held by middle-class women of the era—and reveal those notions about which women appear to have remained ambivalent. As John Cawelti observes, popular writing rests on a "network of assumptions," shared by writer and reader alike. (1976, 33) By examining the basic beliefs that writers affirmed in these books, we can begin to determine the social and ethical values which readers accepted. A close examination of the popular women's novels of the period helps us discern the extent to which ordinary middle-class women of the day were beginning to accept new values and roles. By analyzing incongruities among novelists in their depiction of their female protagonists, we can see which aspects of the "New Woman" were still open to question in the 1920s and 1930s.[1]

Surprisingly little scholarly attention to date has been paid to best-selling women's novels of the interwar period. The study of popular literature in general began with Frank Luther Mott's *Golden Multitudes* (1947) and James D. Hart's *The Popular Book* (1950) which surveyed American popular literature from the colonial period to the mid-twentieth century. A decade later, Russel B. Nye, in *The Unembarrassed Muse* (1970), devoted several chapters to popular literature. All of these studies are more discursive than analytical, which limits their value for the cultural historian. In recent decades, scholars have narrowed their focus to examine best sellers published within a more limited time period, and they have sought to uncover dominant values and attitudes through their analyses of the popular literature of the day. Among the works which have followed this investigative approach are Suzanne Ellery Greene's *Books for Pleasure: Popular Fiction 1914–1945* (1974), Ruth Miller Elson's *Myths and Mores in American Best Sellers, 1865–1965* (1985), and Erik Lofroth's study of best sellers from 1895 to 1920, cited earlier, which is the most successful of these studies at systematically integrating popular literature, social history, and the world view of an era.

While some scholars have explored the broad outlines of popular literature, others have turned their attention more specifically to popular women's literature. Following the lead of Helen Waite Papashvily and, more recently, Nina Baym, cultural historians have begun to examine popular women's fiction of the mid-nineteenth century.[2] A number of scholars, including Jan Cohn, Tania Modelski, and Carol Thurston, have analyzed romance novels of the mid- to late-twentieth century.[3] Others, such as Laura Hapke in *Tales of the Working Girl: Wage-Earning Women in American Literature, 1890–1925* (1992) and Carol Fairbanks, in *Prairie Women: Images in American and Canadian Fiction* (1986), have turned their attention to specific types of popular women's fiction. Although some scholars have included best-selling novels published in the Twenties and Thirties within studies of American best sellers in general or within analyses of popular women's novels in particular, prior to this study none has directly focused their attention on women's best sellers of the interwar era.

The period between the two World Wars is an especially important era in women's social history. In 1920, with the ratification of the Nineteenth Amendment, women got the vote, and some, at least, took advantage of their newly granted right to take an active part in politics. In the Twenties and Thirties, increasing numbers of middle-class women joined their working-class contemporaries in the workplace. While the majority of these new workers were single, quitting their jobs upon marriage, a small but growing minority of middle-class married women stayed on to become "two-job wives," as popular magazine articles described those women who shouldered both work and family responsibilities. Marriage itself was changing by the Twenties and Thirties. The nineteenth-century conception of marriage as an institutionalized arrangement whereby husband and wife were expected to fulfill certain socially defined obligations toward one another was giving way to a more "modern" notion which regarded marriage as a personal relationship between two individuals for the achievement of mutual happiness and emotional fulfillment. Changes in work patterns and marital expectations led inexorably to an increase in the divorce rates. As middle-class women found that they could support themselves and as they came to want more from their husbands than wives had considered their due in the past, there was a rise in the percentage of marriages ending in failure. And as the divorce rate climbed, the widespread censure of those who had chosen to end their marriage in the court abated somewhat.

Despite the fact that these changes exerted relatively constant pressure throughout the interwar era, middle-class women's experiences in the earlier years of this period differed substantially from those later on. While the Twenties was not a decade of prosperity for all, most middle-class Americans experienced good times; for them it was an era of rising expectations. Many young middle-class women could indulge themselves in the activities and products offered by an increasingly commercialized popular culture. This intensified a trend which had its origin in the years before the Great War: a movement toward greater latitude in women's social behavior. Engaging in what was regarded at the time as a "revolution in morals," young women seemed to be casting off Victorian convention by shortening their skirts; bobbing their hair; smoking, drinking, and swearing in public; dancing fast dances; and indiscriminately kissing any and all young men who showed them a good time. The symbol of this "New Woman," of course, was the flapper. While this "revolution" was hardly as thorough-going as contemporary observers feared, there is no question that young women's behavior and attitudes were changing, nor any doubt that this process accelerated in the Twenties.

If the Twenties was a decade in which middle-class women expanded their social boundaries, a period in which the restrictions governing female conduct were relaxed, the Thirties was a time in which these trends were reversed. If the dominant image of the Twenties woman is that of the pleasure-seeking flapper, deftly captured in John Held's magazine cover illustrations; one of the best-remembered image of the Thirties woman is that of the careworn farm woman, caught in Dorothea Lange's "Migrant Mother" photograph. With the onset of the Depression, the material prosperity of the Twenties—enjoyed by some Americans, at least—came abruptly to an end. At best, life became a challenge to be met by hard work and courage, as the pioneers had conquered the wilderness half a century earlier. At worst, life became an insurmountable obstacle, a nightmare which no amount of determination or sacrifice could overcome. In this time of crisis, many Americans renewed their faith in traditional values: women were expected to stay home and take care of their families, not to venture into the workplace where they occupied positions which more rightfully "belonged" to male heads of household. The movement toward broadening the definition of women's roles and status slowed, but the momentum was too great to allow the course of change to come to a complete halt.

It would be a mistake to suggest that the shifts in gender expectations outlined here affected all middle-class women equally during the interwar years. Even in the Twenties, many women remained unswervingly committed to the cult of domesticity, fervent supporters of the notion that a woman's highest calling was that of caring for her home, husband, and children. Many continued to disparage women who ventured into the workplace, especially married women. Many believed that a wife should struggle to preserve her marriage, no matter how dissatisfied she might be, and they refused to condone divorce, regardless of the circumstances precipitating such action. And many were shocked by the "loose" behavior of the flapper—a creature largely created and popularized by the media—which served as a lightning rod for the pervasive disapproval of the social changes of the era.

Even among those who adopted the appearance and mannerisms of the flapper, those who asserted that theirs would be a more "companionate" marriage, those who chose divorce as a solution to their marital difficulties, those who proudly earned their own living—even among all these groups of supposedly "New Women"—acceptance of a "new" set of values and expectations was often contradictory and incomplete. Women's commitment to change varied considerably from individual to individual. Even those who considered themselves "feminists" disagreed as to what goals, exactly, they hoped to achieve. In *The Grounding of Modern Feminism* (1987), Nancy F. Cott describes the efforts of the various women's groups of the Twenties to further the cause of women as hampered by "centrifugal tendencies among women themselves." (266) A central split among feminists occurred over the issue of the Equal Rights Amendment: some supported the amendment on the grounds that women should be considered legally equal to men—in marriage, on the job, and in the courts; others opposed it, arguing that the ERA would invalidate hard-won protective legislation for women. Activists were also divided in their attitudes regarding the sexual "revolution": while many welcomed new norms of sexual permissiveness, more were shocked by such behavior and suspicious that sexual emancipation would cause women to lose "bargaining power, or the right of refusal, a crucial weapon in nineteenth-century sexual politics." (Woloch 1984, 400) If feminists were divided, it should come as no surprise that nonpolitical women, who made up the majority of the female population, found it equally difficult to arrive at mutually satisfactory solutions to the problems they encountered in striving to achieve sexual freedom, fashion more equitable marriages, and balance family and work. Conflict existed not only among women and women's groups but within individuals themselves. Even the most "liberated" women of the Twenties and Thirties found it hard to abandon the traditional notion that a woman's greatest virtue was that of unselfishness. For generations, women had been expected to set aside their own needs and desires in order to satisfy those of others. To act in a way which society perceived as self-centered was difficult indeed, as this was the one charge above all others which women sought to avoid.

One place where the changes in women's conduct and values, in all their complexity and contradictions, was being explored was in best-selling women's novels. Published in hardcover editions and often serialized in women's magazines, these novels were written by such popular women writers as Kathleen Norris, Bess Streeter Aldrich, Edna Ferber, and Fannie Hurst. Although little information exists as to the gender of the readers of these best sellers, it is likely that women constituted the bulk of the audience for most popular novels, especially those written by women. A study of library-borrowers conducted in the Thirties found that the best-selling authors of the day had a much larger following among female readers, especially housewives, than among male readers. (Lofroth 1983, 17) While no contemporary investigations of the readers of popular fiction in the Twenties have been undertaken, Twenties literary critics and popular novelists themselves seem to have assumed that the best-selling novels by women were read primarily by other women. One reviewer recommended Susan Ertz' *Nina* in 1921 by predicting that "[e]very woman will be charmed with this novel because it is veracious in its feminine psychology, as most novels by men are not." (*Booklist*, April 1921, 241) Another remarked of Dorothy Canfield's *The Home-Maker* that the "reader's interest in the book will depend largely upon his—or perhaps it would be better to say her—sympathy with the author's point of view." (*New York Times*, May 25, 1924, 22) Of Temple Bailey's *Blue Window*, the *New York World* sniffed, "There are worse books published for the feminine masses. . . but not much worse." (April 11, 1926, 7) The *New York Tribune* wrote of Mary Roberts Rinehart's *Lost Ecstasy*, "It is a woman's story and there is too much in it of 'what every woman knows' to make it quite comfortable reading for men." (June 19, 1927, 10)

If women were the primary audience for these books, what kind of women were they? It seems likely that most of them were middle-class. In his study of American best sellers, Erik Lofroth reminds us that best-seller lists were compiled from sales figures obtained from the nation's largest bookstores, retail outlets predominately patronized "more by upper and middle income groups than by lower." (1983, 17) When the works of popular novelists like Kathleen Norris or Temple Bailey appeared in women's magazines, it was those periodicals aimed at middle-class women—*Ladies' Home Journal, The Delineator, Good Housekeeping*, and *Woman's Home Companion*—in which these writers chose to place their short stories and novels, not in the confession magazines which had largely working-class readerships. (Makosky 1966, 12)

Proceeding on the assumption that readers bought the novels featuring the heroines whom they most admired or with whom they could best empathize and embodying plot structures and themes which had some resonance with regard to their own lives and expectations, what are these fictional characters and plots like? This book will attempt to answer this question by examining novels featuring female protagonists and written by best-selling women authors. With few exceptions, the writers included in this study are American.[4] Most of the novels analyzed in the following chapters appeared in *The Bookman*'s yearly best-seller lists during the Twenties or in the yearly lists compiled by *Publishers' Weekly* in the Thirties. Based upon sales figures submitted by selected bookshops and department stores across the country, these lists indicate the ten top-selling works of fiction for the year. Some of the novels discussed in this study did not sell sufficient copies to attain yearly best-seller status; they did, however, appear on *The Bookman* or *Publishers' Weekly* best-seller lists compiled for each month.[5] Some of the women who wrote best-selling novels were quite prolific, often producing one or more books a year. This paper will examine additional works by these best-selling authors even though these books may not have sold well enough to become best sellers themselves.

The books included in this study, then, are those which were best sellers in their own right and/or were produced by the best-selling novelists of the day. Their popularity, measured by their sales figures, arguably indicates that they represent the interests and tastes of a significant proportion of middle-class women of the era; thus, it is appropriate to examine in some detail the values and assumptions presented in these widely-read novels.

It would be a mistake, however, to regard these books merely as reflecting popular values and assumptions. Of equal or perhaps greater significance is the fact that these novels are likely to have shaped as well as reflected women's attitudes. And, by and large, popular women's novels promoted a conservative agenda regarding gender roles.[6] In an era in which women's roles and values were being renegotiated, the best-selling novels of the day depicted unsophisticated "flappers" whose deepest desire was to marry and raise a family, women who sacrificed their happiness for the men they loved, young matrons who strove to save their marriage regardless of personal cost, and frontierswomen who battled wild animals, drought, blizzards, and despair for the sake of their family. Regardless of variations in regional background or historical setting, despite differences in class or age, the heroines of best-selling women's novels are consistently depicted as caring and unselfish, placing the needs of their family before their own.

In the chapters that follow, I shall attempt to trace the various conceptions of women reflected in these popular novels and to interpret the values and assumptions expressed in these best sellers in the light of the social history of women in the interwar era. In chapter one, I examine the manner in which the young unmarried woman, particularly the flapper, is portrayed in women's popular novels in the Twenties. Women who came to maturity in this decade have been thought to have discarded the conventions of the previous generation. While some best sellers written by women support this interpretation, the majority suggest that young women assumed, at most, only a veneer of "modernity," adopting new dress and hairstyles and affecting slightly more daring sexual behavior—yet remaining as firmly committed to recreating traditional gender roles as did their mothers before them.

In chapter two, I analyze popular women novelists' treatment of marriage. While Dorothy Canfield promotes marital equality in her novels, most writers of the Twenties and Thirties continue to reaffirm the "cult of domesticity," presenting heroines who devote themselves to keeping house, raising children, and comforting husbands in exchange for their spouses' financial support and protection.

Given their position on marriage, it follows that most best-selling women writers are opposed to divorce, the subject of chapter three. Kathleen Norris, for example, asserts that divorce is out of the question, that it is the woman's responsibility to hold her marriage together, no matter how much pain it may cause her to do so. Thirties novelist Margaret Ayer Barnes echoes Norris' message, albeit more subtly. Like Barnes, Edith Wharton frequently deals with the topic of divorce in her novels and short stories. While Wharton tends to be sympathetic to her divorced women characters in her earlier fiction, by the Twenties she is more apt to defend the institution of marriage and to dramatize the dangers of dissolving matrimonial ties through divorce—a position not far removed from that of Barnes, or even Norris.

In chapter four, I examine popular women writers' handling of working women. While most novelists reflect societal acceptance of middle-class single women in the workplace, few women writers of the period regard married women working as "natural" and few support protagonists who choose to pursue a career at the expense of marriage. Even in Fannie Hurst's *Imitation of Life* (1933), Bea Chipley's astounding business success hardly compensates for her inability to marry the man she loves and to retire from business to become a full-time homemaker.

In chapter five, I discuss farm novels which feature female protagonists. A surprisingly large number of such novels, either set in the present or focused upon the pioneer experience of America's frontier past, were published in the Twenties and Thirties. In general, farm and pioneer novels tend to valorize social mobility while questioning the era's growing emphasis upon materialism and the consumer ethic. While Willa Cather, Ellen Glasgow, and Edna Ferber created heroines who were among the most independent female characters portrayed in popular women's novels of the day, other writers of farm and pioneer books, such as Bess Streeter Aldrich and Gladys Hasty Carroll, tended to privilege a conservative interpretation of women's roles and expectations, creating heroines who accept their place as mothers and housewives and who have no desire to compete with men on their own ground.

In chapter six, I examine the nature of heroines and antiheroines drawn by best-selling women writers and conclude that the fundamental distinction between the two types is that the heroine is compassionate and selfless, while the antiheroine is calculating and self-centered. The heroine is willing to sacrifice her happiness for the sake of her loved ones, while the antiheroine lives only to satisfy her own needs and desires. Novel after novel highlights the heroine's virtues by setting them against her foil's failings. Nowhere is this contrast more evident than in Daphne du Maurier's *Rebecca* (1938), a book in which the nameless heroine's innocence and unselfishness are contrasted with the dead Rebecca's sophistication and self-indulgence. Virtually alone among women's best sellers of the period, Margaret Mitchell's *Gone with the Wind* (1936) features a secondary character who possesses the traits usually associated with the heroine, while the protagonist has the ruthlessness and self-absorption commonly the property of the antiheroine. Scarlett O'Hara's self-interest and lack of feminine refinement enable her to survive in a chaotic and threatening world, but they cause her to forfeit her chance to achieve the prize with which more conventional heroines are usually rewarded: at the end of the novel, Scarlett loses Rhett Butler, the only man—she finally realizes—whom she has ever truly loved. As unusual a heroine as Scarlett appears to be when judged by the fictional norms of the Twenties and Thirties, she is less unique when compared to more recent best-seller heroines, many of whom resemble Scarlett O'Hara much more closely than they do Melanie Wilkes.

YESTERDAY'S STORIES

CHAPTER ONE

The Flapper and Her Sisters

In the 1920s, as historian Paula Fass observes in *The Damned and the Beautiful: American Youth in the 1920's* (1977), young men and women challenged the conventions and mores of their parents' generation. They danced fast dances, drank whiskey from hip flasks, petted in the backseats of motorcars, and sneered at the aspirations and life-style of their elders. Their apparently iconoclastic behavior prompted conservative social critics to denounce them as a threat to the established social order. Young women received more than their share of opprobrium. The "flapper," with her bobbed hair, shortened skirts, rouged lips, and cigarette cases, became the symbol of the hedonism, the indifference to traditional standards, and the unrestrained sexuality which conservatives believed to be characteristic of the young women of the era. "Gazing at the young women of the period," Fass writes,

the traditionalist saw the end of American civilization as he had known it. Its firm and robust outlines, best symbolized by the stable mother secure in her morality and content in her home, were pushed aside and replaced by the giddy flapper, rouged and clipped, careening in a drunken stupor to the lewd strains of a jazz quartet. (25)

Popular women novelists of the decade could scarcely have been unaware of the flapper and her critics. The flapper "phenomenon" was the subject of scores of magazine articles, movies frequently featured "jazz age" heroines, and young women's appearance and conduct was the topic of dinner table conversation in countless dining rooms across the country. In their fictional treatment of young women in their books, women novelists both reflected widespread changes in female attitudes and behavior in the postwar era and implicitly commented upon these trends. A close analysis of young female protagonists in popular women's novels of the Twenties indicates that most fictional flappers, like many of their real-life sisters, were more traditional at heart than their breezy demeanor—and F. Scott Fitzgerald's depictions of flappers—led observers to believe.[1] Nevertheless, there is enough diversity among the various best-selling women's novelists in their treatment of young female characters, especially with regard to the expression of sexuality, to indicate that in some ways the nature of the middle-class woman was being contested, was in the process of redefinition. In particular, middle-class women were beginning to assert themselves as sexual beings, with sexual needs as legitimate as those of men.

Some best-selling women writers were quick to draw upon the trend toward more liberal sexual attitudes in creating young female protagonists. As I have argued elsewhere, even though English writer E. M. Hull's depiction of an apparently independent and self-sufficient female conquered by a masterful lover in *The Sheik* (1921) appears to reflect a conservative reaction against women's attempts to redefine their status and roles in contemporary society, at the same time, Hull's novel strongly hints that in at least one area, the bedroom, women could now be perceived as the equals of men. As sexual beings, women, like men, could openly and unashamedly enjoy intimate physical relations with their partners. (Raub 1992) Hull's protagonist Diana Mayo is affected by her captor's sensuality from the very start: when he first embraces her, "the truth of his scorching lips, the clasp of his arms, the close union of his warm, strong body robbed her of all strength, of all power of resistance." His kiss is "like a narcotic, drugging her almost into insensibility." (Hull 1921, 58) Once she discovers that she loves him, she finds it harder and harder to "make a show of reluctance when she was longing to give unreservedly." (146) Finally her passions overwhelm her, and "for the first time she surrendered to him wholly, clinging to him passionately, and giving him kiss for kiss with an absolute abandon of all resistance." (148)

The Sheik was one of the few novels of the decade to make the American best-seller list two years in a row, ranking sixth among the top ten best-selling works of fiction in 1921 and rising to second place in 1922. In 1921, Paramount produced a silent film version of the story, also titled *The Sheik* and starring Rudolph Valentino in his first successful and best-remembered role.[2] The movie was as popular with movie audiences as the book was with readers, and the word "sheik" entered the American language as a slang expression referring to a man with sex appeal.

Another popular novel of the decade also featured a passionate and sensual heroine. *Wild Geese* (1925), winner of a prize offered by the Pictorial Review, the Dodd, Mead Company, and the Famous Players-Lasky Corporation, was written by Martha Ostenso, a writer of magazine stories and novels. Born in Norway in 1900, she emigrated with her parents to America when she was two. During her childhood her family lived in a succession of small towns in Minnesota and South Dakota and eventually settled in Manitoba, Canada. She later wrote that it was "during a summer vacation from my university work . . . that I went into the lake district of Manitoba, well toward the frontier of that northern civilization. My novel, *Wild Geese*, lay there, waiting to be put into words. Here was human nature stark, unattired in the convention of a smoother, softer life." (Kunitz and Haycraft 1942, 1059) In *Wild Geese*, Ostenso presents Judith Gare, the hot-blooded daughter of a cruel and repressive father. When she becomes old enough to become aware of the urges of her body, Judith submits to her feelings. In an early scene, she is alone in the woods. Ostenso writes:

It was clingingly warm, as before rain. Not knowing fully what she was doing, Judith took off all her clothing and lay flat on the damp ground with the waxy feeling of new, sunless vegetation under her. (66)

Judith's sexual desires become more focused when Sven Sandbo returns to the area. The first time Judith sees Sven, she knows that he is watching her riding her colt and she is "conscious of the picture she made, magnificently riding." (97) The second time they meet, Judith feels a strong physical attraction for Sven. Filled with an uncontrollable desire for him, she begins to wrestle with Sven—and Ostenso devotes two full pages to a graphic description of their struggle. The author concludes this passage by writing:

Her panting body heaved against his as they lay full length on the ground locked in furious embrace. Judith buried her nails in the flesh over his breast, beat her knees into his loins, set her teeth in the more tender skin over the veins at his wrists. . . . Sven's breath fell in hot gusts on Judith's face. . . . Sven released the arm that he had bent to the breaking point. He was trembling.
"Judie," he muttered. "Judie—look at me." Judith raised her eyelids slowly. "Kiss me—now," she said in a breath. (118)

Matters do not end with a kiss. Judith gets pregnant. She and Sven secretly make plans to elope after the haying is finished, but their arrangements become unnecessary when her dictatorial father is killed in a fire at the end of the novel.

Judith Gare is depicted as a woman who is scarcely more inhibited by social conventions than is her colt. In abandoning herself to her physical desires, she breaks more decisively with the restraints imposed upon women than does Diana Mayo, who reacts to rather than acts upon her feelings. Diana responds to the Sheik's caresses, but she does not have to assume responsibility for her behavior: she is cast in the traditional female role of victim; she is not taking on the male role of aggressor. Judith, on the other hand, is not forced into physical intimacy with Sven; she enters willingly into their wrestling match, and it is she who demands that he kiss her. Ostenso's steamy treatment of Judith's sexual awakening did not succeed in making *Wild Geese* the runaway best seller that *The Sheik* had become. Ostenso's novels were never more than minor successes, appearing briefly on the monthly lists of best-selling novels but not on the yearly lists. Ostenso's shaky character development and her use of improbable and melodramatic plot devices may have limited her popularity: critics of her books objected to the "theatrical action and the pompous prose" (*Saturday Review*, October 15, 1927, 197) and to her "conception of character which is undeniably sentimental and a little false." (*New York Times*, September 1, 1929, 7) At the same time, readers may well have felt uneasy with Ostenso's rendering of female passion.

A more popular novel of the Twenties than *Wild Geese* portrays a protagonist who, like Judith Gare, is not reticent about initiating sexual encounters. With the help of her love-charm, Julia Peterkin's Scarlet Sister Mary, in the 1928 best-selling novel of the same title, deliberately entices a whole succession of men to her bed. Mary is a black woman who lives in the Quarters at the Blue Brook Plantation on the coast of South Carolina. When the story opens, she is fifteen," a slender, darting, high-spirited girl, a leader of the young set" who is about to marry July, "perhaps the wildest young buck in the Quarters." (15) For the first months of their married life, they are happy together, but soon after the birth of their first child, July starts seeing another woman. Mary goes to old Daddy Cudjoe to get a charm to win back July's affections but before she can use it he leaves her. As the days and weeks go by with no sign of July, Mary grieves and pines. She loses her strength and her looks. Finally, she rallies. She turns to her love-charm. With its help, she conceives her second child, a daughter by July's brother June.

Fifteen years pass. Through judicious use of her love-charm, Mary now has nine children, all of different fathers. Mary's satisfaction with her unconventional life-style is shattered when her first child Unex abruptly dies. Fearing that God is punishing her for her sinful life, Mary goes into the woods, prays, and has a vision. The deacons decide that she has had a geniune conversion and welcome her back into the church. They would not perhaps have been so quick to readmit her had they overheard her conversation with Daddy Cudjoe after the church meeting. When he asks for his love-charm back, assuming that the reformed Mary will need it no longer, she refuses to return it: "I'll lend em to you when you need em, Daddy, but I couldn't gi way my love-charm. E's all I got now to keep me young." (345)

Scarlet Sister Mary was written by the daughter of a prominent South Carolinian physician whose wife died soon after her daughter's birth. Julia Peterkin was raised by a black nurse, and as a child she spoke both standard English and the Gullah dialect of her "Mauma." In 1903, shortly after graduating from college, she married William Peterkin, whose family owned and operated one of the largest and most productive plantations in the state. As mistress of the estate, she came into daily contact with the four to five hundred black workers on the plantation. Mrs. Peterkin began writing seriously after 1920, at the age of forty. She took as her subject the Gullah blacks and their culture. While her early efforts were generally applauded by both black and white critics, it was not until the appearance of *Scarlet Sister Mary* in 1928 that she achieved popular success as well. Awarded the Pulitzer Prize for the best novel of the year and later the vehicle for Ethel Barrymore's "first and not altogether successful experiment in playing black face" on the stage (Kunitz and Haycraft 1942, 1097), the book eventually sold over a million copies. The late Twenties was a propitious time for bringing out a novel set in a black community. The Harlem Renaissance was in full swing, and both black and white writers were winning acclaim for their portrayal of African-American life.[3]

There is no doubt that the novel's heroine is accepting of extramarital sex; yet, we should not read too much into Mary's example. One reviewer wrote that *Scarlet Sister Mary* "evidently presents an authentic picture of Negro life, standards, morals, viewpoint, and character close to the soil."(*Springfield Republican*, December 9, 1928, 7) The operative word in this review is "Negro": it is precisely because Mary is a woman of color that middle-class white readers could permit her greater latitude of action than they would be likely to condone in white protagonists. White critics and, presumably, readers saw Mary and her people as "exotics," as children of nature, "close to the soil" and premoral in their standards. Black poet Ruth G. Dixon commented upon this phenomenon in a poem published in *The Crisis* in 1930. Addressing her verses "To the lovers of 'Porgy,' 'Scarlet Sister Mary,' and other stories 'characteristic' of Negro life," Dixon remarks:

> You cry "Eureka!" and rejoice
> You've found at last the Negro!
> Primitive! Beautiful! Untarnished
> By the light of your civilization,
> Unfettered by your laws
> Of social decency.
> (Quoted in Honey 1989, 83)

In some ways, Diana Mayo, Judith Gare, and Scarlet Sister Mary are all "unfettered" by the "laws of social decency." The action of *The Sheik* takes place beyond the boundaries of "civilization," where the conventions do not apply; Judith Gare is a child of nature, a homegrown exotic whose story is told sympathetically but with some degree of distance by a more traditional heroine, the new schoolteacher who is boarding with the Gares; and Mary is a member of a "primitive" race of people whose mores are not expected to conform to those of conventional white society.

When we turn our attention to popular heroines who seem to be more typical of young middle-class white women of the Twenties, we find at least a few who appear to have broken as completely with the conventions of the past as have the three atypical heroines described above. The best known of these protagonists is Lorelei Lee in Hollywood screenwriter Anita Loos' first work of fiction, "Gentlemen Prefer Blondes," which first ran in installments in *Harper's Bazaar* in 1925. Illustrated by the celebrated Ralph Barton, the story was hugely popular. The book was even more successful. A publisher friend of Loos first brought out a small "vanity edition" of fifteen hundred copies which sold out the very day it reached the bookstores. A second edition of sixty thousand copies sold out nearly as quickly. As Loos recalled,"I believe the book ran into forty-five editions before the early demand had ceased." (1925, xv) The novel rose to second place on the best-seller list for 1926. In the fall of 1926, a stage production of the story began a six-month run in New York. Two years later Paramount released a film based on the best seller. In 1953, Howard Hawks directed a remake of the 1928 movie, starring Marilyn Monroe and Jane Russell.[4] It was Monroe's performance in this film classic which established Lorelei Lee firmly in the popular imagination as the archetypal flapper.

The story starts in New York and follows dizzy blonde Lorelei Lee and her brunette friend Dorothy on a tour of Europe—paid for by Lorelei's gentleman friend Mr. Eisman, known in Chicago as "the Button King." (Loos 1925, 12) Rather foolishly, Mr. Eisman leaves Lorelei and Dorothy to make most of the trip on their own, and Lorelei turns a number of male heads along the way, trading sexual favors for expensive gifts. Eventually, on a train to Vienna, Lorelei meets Henry Spoffard, scion of an old and wealthy Philadelphian family—and a bachelor. She wastes no time in setting her cap for him, despite the fact that Spoffard and his mother disapprove of the kind of fast living that is Lorelei's trademark. With an eye for the main chance, Lorelei instantly changes her demeanor. A consummate actress who believes in giving her public what it wants, Lorelei immerses herself in her new role and remains in character even in the privacy of her diary. In it, she writes that Henry has never married

because his mother does not think that all of the flappers we seem to have nowadays are what a young man ought to marry when a young man is full of so many morals as Mr. Spoffard seems to be full of. So I told Mr. Spoffard that I really felt just like his mother about all of the flappers because I am an old fashioned girl. (139)

Henry proposes and Lorelei accepts. After their marriage they move to Hollywood, where Spoffard finances movies in which Lorelei stars. Everyone, including Lorelei, is happy, and she concludes her diary, "feeling that, after all, everything always turns out for the best." (217)

If we point to *"Gentlemen Prefer Blondes"* as evidence, it certainly appears that women's values and behavior were undergoing dramatic change in the Twenties. Lorelei Lee may pretend to be an old-fashioned girl, but she is a flapper through and through. The Barton illustrations show an attractive young woman, with bobbed hair, rouged lips, and short skirts. Lorelei has none of the traditional feminine reticence concerning sex. Lorelei is a professional gold digger, ready to take what she can get, to sell her sexual charms to the highest bidder. Seldom romantic but always materialistic, Lorelei writes in her diary that "kissing your hand may make you feel very very good but a diamond and safire [sic] bracelet lasts forever." (100) Like a conventional woman's novel, "Gentlemen Prefer Blondes" ends with matrimony; yet, "Gentlemen Prefer Blondes" is hardly a conventional woman's novel, and Lorelei is scarcely about to settle down to a life of domestic bliss. She has established herself in Hollywood, where she is beginning a new career in which she can charm men en masse instead of one at a time.

Popular though it undoubtedly was, "Gentlemen Prefer Blondes" should not be regarded as a typical women's novel of the Twenties. Firstly, Anita Loos was a screenwriter and playwright by profession and a popular novelist only by accident, a novelist, moreover, whose single best seller owes no debts to the traditions which shape the plot, characterization, and tone of other popular women's novels of the decade. Secondly, "Gentlemen Prefer Blondes" was intended and received as a farce. Irritated that H. L. Mencken preferred a "witless blonde" over her brunette self, Anita Loos allegedly wrote the story as a joke at Mencken's expense. Mencken called Loos the "first American writer ever to make fun of sex!" (Quoted in Loos 1977, 77) Unlike the protagonists of other women's novels, Lorelei Lee was not meant to be taken seriously.[5]

Totally different in mood from the lighthearted "Gentlemen Prefer Blondes" is the darker Ex-Wife, published in 1929 by magazine writer Ursula Parrott. Nevertheless, the two books do have a superficial similarity. Like Loos' novel, Ex-Wife is written in the first person, a relatively uncommon novelistic format for fiction of the day. Like Lorelei Lee, Parrott's heroine Patricia (who is not given a last name) is a thoroughly liberated young lady: Patricia drinks alcohol, frequents Manhattan speakeasies and Harlem nightclubs, smokes cigarettes, uses profanity upon occasion, wears makeup, and dresses in the latest styles. While Loos only implies that Lorelei has sex with men in return for diamond bracelets and the like, Parrott is explicit in informing the reader that Patricia sleeps with a succession of lovers. More innocent, perhaps, than Lorelei, Patricia refuses to accept gifts from those who share her bed: refusing a present from a would-be lover, Patricia reflects that the "only thing I have left to cherish is my amateur standing." (174)

Ex-Wife, which sold one hundred thousand copies, was a "succès de scandale," as Parrott's son recalled some sixty years later. (M. L. Parrott 1989, 219) Yet, Patricia becomes a "loose" woman against her will. Following her confession of a single episode of infidelity, her husband Peter rejects her. Patricia devotes a good deal of effort to winning him back, a goal with which few readers today would be likely to empathize, given Peter's own marital faithlessness and his brutal physical abuse of his wife—on one occasion he hits her across the mouth and on another he pushes her through a glass door. As an "anaesthetic" to assuage the grief she experiences when her husband leaves her, Patricia moves through a series of one-night stands. Patricia may be sexually liberated, but she is certainly not a feminist. In fact, as one of the few women novelists of the day to comment directly on feminist politics, Parrott, through Patricia's friend Lucia, blames the women's movement for the plight of Patricia and ex-wives like her:

We are *free*. Applesauce! Free to pay our own rent, and buy our own clothes, and put up with the eccentricities of three to eight men who have authority over us in business, instead of having to please just one husband. . . .
   Women used to have status, a relative security. Now they have the status of any prostitute, success while their looks hold out. If the next generation of women have any sense, they'll dynamite the statue of Susan B. Anthony, and start a crusade for the revival of chivalry. (Parrott 1929, 70)

Eventually, Patricia recovers from the breakup of her marriage, stops sleeping around, falls in love with a married man and renounces him for the sake of his family, and remarries on the rebound, promising her new husband rather wearily that she means to make him a "perfect wife." (218)
   Although some of its action seems contrived, the emotional tone of *Ex-Wife* seems genuine. Despite the fact that one reviewer complained that the book had "neither sociological nor literary value" (*Springfield Republican*, August 25, 1929, 7), another was so taken by the psychological realism of the novel that this reviewer assumed the book was based upon the author's own life, writing that *Ex-Wife* was a "sincerely written autobiography, presented as fiction." (*Bookman*, September 1929, xx) Another judged that the "narrative seems to be authentic: it has a certain intangible quality of truth." (*Nation*, September 18, 1929, 310) Yet another promised readers that "you can learn about women" from Parrott's novel. (*New York Herald Tribune*, August 11,1929, 6)
   In spite of the striking difference in tone between the two novels, the reviewer for the *Herald Tribune* associated Parrott's book with Loos', claiming that *Ex-Wife* "has about the same fidelity to life as 'Gentlemen Prefer Blondes.' " It appears that what this book critic meant by "fidelity to life" was simply both authors' willingness to discuss, in the critic's words, "casual immoralities [with] unabashed frankness." (*New York Herald Tribune*, August 11, 1929, 6) Both books, of course, do feature heroines who are relatively unconstrained by conventional sexual standards. That Parrott's novel lacks the lighter touch of Loos' book probably accounts for the fact that *Ex-Wife* never matched *"Gentlemen Prefer Blondes"* in sales figures. While Parrott's descriptions of her heroine's love-trysts were hardly as

vivid as Ostenso's depictions of Judith Gare's sexual encounters, perhaps readers nevertheless felt uncomfortable with so blatantly promiscuous—and so bitterly rendered—a heroine. As the reviewer for *Bookman* perceptively remarked of *Ex-Wife*, "[b]eneath the alluring glamour of . . . [sexual] freedom can be felt the hopeless despair of wrecked ideals." (*Bookman*, September 1929, xx) *Ex-Wife* was hardly the novel with which to curl up on the sofa and while away an idle hour.

It is important to note that the more sexually liberated heroine was the exception rather than the rule in fiction written by popular women novelists in the Twenties. While most middle-class women readers may have read *The Sheik* and *"Gentlemen Prefer Blondes"*—or seen the movies—the fictional flappers with which they were more familiar were those created by such well-known women writers as Temple Bailey, Gene Stratton-Porter, and, especially, Kathleen Norris. Unlike Anita Loos or Julia Peterkin, each of whom produced only one major best seller, and unlike Martha Ostenso or Ursula Parrott, whose books never sold in sufficient quantities to enable them to enter the ranks of top best-selling writers, authors like Bailey, Stratton-Porter, and Norris churned out one best seller after another, attracting and cultivating a loyal readership who remained faithful to them throughout their long careers. While readers may have maintained their distance from the burlesque of a Lorelei Lee, the primitivism of a Scarlet Sister Mary, or the exoticism of Diana Mayo's plight; they could perhaps more closely identify with the melodrama of a Kathleen Norris or Temple Bailey character, whose background, behavior, and values seemed more akin to their own.

More typical of the fictional heroines of the Twenties than Diana Mayo or Lorelei Lee were those created by Gene Stratton-Porter, one of the most popular women novelists of the era, who was known for her nature books and her editorials on *McCall's* "Gene Stratton-Porter Page" as well as for her novels. At the time of her death in 1924, more than ten million copies of her books had been sold—and four more books were published after her death. (Overton 1928, 312)[6] Beginning with *The Harvester* in 1911 and concluding with the posthumously published *Keeper of the Bees* in 1925, six of her twelve novels made the best-seller list, ranking among the top ten works of fiction for the year in terms of sales. Stratton-Porter was one of the first popular novelists to see her books recreated on film: over twenty movies were made from her novels—many produced by the author's own movie production company, Gene Stratton-Porter Productions, which she formed "to protect the moralistic tone of her work." (Bakerman 1979, 180)

Stratton-Porter established the pattern for her heroines with her depiction of Elnora Comstock in *A Girl of the Limberlost*, published in 1909, and the characterization of her protagonists remained virtually unchanged thereafter. Wholesome, sensible, and beautiful, Elnora is also compassionate, self-reliant, and intelligent: "There was no form of suffering with which the girl could not sympathize, no work she was afraid to attempt, no subject she had investigated she did not understand." (130) When the handsome young hero arrives on the scene, he is immediately captivated by Elnora, even though he is already claimed by a physically attractive but selfish society girl. Elnora's virtue wins her the hero. Association with Elnora prompts the society girl to reform: she vows to be more like Elnora in the future.

While one would hardly expect Stratton-Porter to portray the heroine of her 1909 novel as a flapper, it is perhaps surprising that in *Her Father's Daughter*, published in 1921, the novelist presents a protagonist whose virtues and behavior are equally old-fashioned. Seventeen-year-old Linda Strong lives with her older sister Eileen. Linda is unaffected, honest, resourceful, and highly patriotic. More interested in getting good grades and continuing her late father's nature studies than in attracting male attention, she defends her unfashionable clothing as "practical." Eileen, on the other hand, has succumbed to modern fashion. Flapper-like, she wears her dresses short, smokes—in secret—and uses makeup; but her behavior only proves her capacity for deception. As Linda remarks:

I never knew Eileen to be honest about anything in her life unless the truth served her better than an evasion. Her hair was not honest color and it was not honest curl. Her eyebrows were not so dark as she made them. Her cheeks and lips were not so red . . . her form was not so perfect. Her friends were selected because they could serve her. (26)

By the end of the novel, Eileen has reformed somewhat, but it is the natural Linda, not the artificial Eileen, who has captured the most eligible bachelor. Stratton-Porter is topical in her inclusion of a flapper in her cast of characters, but, although she acknowledges the "revolution" in female appearance and behavior underway by the early Twenties, she refuses to make any concession to it; it is the "old-fashioned" female who triumphs in the end—by eliciting a marriage proposal from the most eligible male character in the novel.[7]

Temple Bailey's heroines seem equally as unsophisticated in their behavior and outlook as do Stratton-Porter's. Bailey began her literary career writing stories for women's magazines and later turned to novels. *The Dim Lantern* and *The Blue Window* appeared on the yearly best-seller lists for 1923 and 1926, respectively, and another half-dozen Bailey romances were reported among the monthly best sellers during the decade. In 1942, the editors of *Twentieth Century Authors* estimated that "at least three million of her books, including reprints, have been sold, and her readers must be reckoned at many millions more, since nearly half these sales are made to circulating libraries." (Kunitz and Haycraft, 61)

Bailey is only slightly more accepting of new manners and styles in the behavior of young women than is Stratton-Porter. Jane Barnes in *The Dim*

Lantern (1923) has some of the attributes of a flapper, as her "bobbed hair emphasized the boyish effect of her straight, slim figure." (10) Nevertheless, "Jane might have bobbed hair, but she did not have a bobbed-hair mind." (135) The author portrays her as having "old-fashioned domestic qualities." (135) She keeps the house spic and span, cooks for her brother, and economically mends and remends her old frocks. She dreams of marrying, settling down in a snug little house, with a little garden, and raising a family. By the end of the novel, her dream has come true. It is her old-fashioned charm which has won the heart of the hero.

Bailey's other novels are remarkably similar to *Dim Lantern* in characterization and plot. Her heroines are all "child-women." In *The Blue Window* (1926), Hildegarde Carew's charm for one suitor "lay . . . in a sort of quaint childishness, in her hot little tempers, her quick repentances. She was so utterly herself, without affectation." (95) In *Wallflowers* (1927), Rufus Fiske thinks of Sandra Claybourne as a "little girl, with . . . engaging charms of youth and *naïveté*." (109) Bailey surrounds her heroines with an assortment of sophisticated young women, thus highlighting her protagonists' freshness and lack of artifice. As in Stratton-Porter's novels, the more "worldly" female characters are clearly on the wrong track. In *Wallflowers*, Stephanie Moore is "delightful to look at, delicate, sophisticated, with a thousand subtle perfections," (112) but in Bailey's lexicon, sophistication and subtlety are not positive female attributes. Stephanie deliberately pursues Gale Markham, even stooping to tell him, untruthfully, that Theodora Claybourne is engaged to another man. In the end, Stephanie's machinations fail, and the reader is left with the decided impression that Stephanie has only herself to blame for losing the man she loves to her rival. In *The Blue Window*, Sally Hulbert appears at first to be another Stephanie Moore: "Sally, with her impertinences, and revealing franknesses . . . with her copper-colored bob, and her lip-stick" (1926, 113) seems merely a foil for the ingenuous Hildegarde. It turns out that Sally is more traditional than she appears. When she finally marries the man of her dreams, she writes Hildegarde to say that "each day I am falling more in love with him. Which sounds as brazen as a brass band, but it isn't. A wife should love her husband—and I am as meek as they make 'em. Old-fashioned." (318)

For the Bailey heroine, life consists of passively waiting and hoping for marriage to the right man. (Only the villainesses view the situation as a contest between rivals for the affections of the hero. The villainess deliberately schemes to ensnare the man of her choice; the heroine, meanwhile, gains the heart of the hero by remaining above the fray.) The Bailey heroine spends her time falling in love, being separated from her truelove for a variety of fairly minor reasons, being pursued by wealthy suitors who can offer her riches but not happiness, and finally being reunited with her beloved and entering into a life of marital bliss.

Love, in a Bailey novel, has little hint of physical passion. The Bailey heroine refuses even to kiss a suitor until she has accepted his hand in marriage. Crispin Harlow, Hildegarde's childhood sweetheart in *The Blue Window*, wants to kiss her good-bye when she moves away from home. He assures her, " 'It won't tie you to anything. But it will make you remember that I—care.' She stood very still, then: 'Crispin, it would tie me—I mustn't.' " (22)

Somewhat more demonstrative in their affections—toward the "right" man—are the heroines created by Kathleen Norris, an even more popular novelist than either Gene Stratton-Porter or Temple Bailey. Over a career spanning five decades, Norris produced eighty-one novels, two autobiographies, and scores of short stories and magazine articles. Her first novel to appear on the best-seller lists was *The Heart of Rachael*, which ranked tenth in sales among works of fiction for 1916. Four years later, *Harriet and the Piper* (1920) was also tenth in fiction sales for the year. At least a dozen Norris novels were monthly best sellers during the Twenties and early Thirties, the period of Norris' greatest popularity. Fourteen years after her death in 1966, a biographer observed that "Kathleen Norris was one of the most popular and commercially successful authors of her time, her books selling ten million copies." (Richey 1980, 510)

Like Bailey, Norris is somewhat more receptive to postwar changes in young women's appearance and behavior than Gene Stratton-Porter; thus, Norris creates heroines of the Twenties who take on at least some of the characteristics of the flapper. Nevertheless, Norris tends to incorporate the flavor but not the substance of the flapper in her protagonists. It is probable that Norris' moderation in her depiction of the flapper contributed to her popularity in a decade in which public opinion of new modes of behavior was sharply divided. As film historian Kevin Brownlow has remarked, "[t]he conflict [over moral behavior] was particularly harsh in the twenties, for Victorians and religious fundamentalists were living in the same communities with flappers and their sheiks. The [movie] industry had the impossible task of appealing to both extremes"—and so did popular novelists. (1990, 29) Thus, Norris' heroines bob their hair and wear short dresses. They even return young men's kisses, sometimes with passion, as does Juanita Espinosa in *The Sea Gull* (1927). Norris writes:

Juanita, not knowing what she did, raised her face, in the dim gloom, and Kent bent to her for his first kiss. And for a long minute they clung so, the girl's slender body close to his, their hearts beating together, and all the world whirling about Juanita in a storm of ecstasy and fear and joy. (154)

But those characters who defy the moral strictures of their elders come to regret their actions. In *The Foolish Virgin* (1929), Pamela Raleigh's mother predicts darkly that Pamela is riding for a fall:

[N]o chaperons. . . . Drivin' about with boys in speed cars, smokin'—when I kissed you now all I could smell on yo' hair was smoke—drinkin'—I tell you, Pam, it's dangerous an' it's bad, an' the time's comin' when you're going to see it like I do. (5)

All too soon, Pamela discovers that her mother is right. Late one Saturday night she goes driving with Chester Hilliard. Seventeen miles from town they run out of gas and are forced to spend the night in an abandoned cabin. Although they are innocent of sexual wrongdoing, Pamela is ostracized from polite society. She is forced to take a job as companion and helper on a country ranch, where her newfound seriousness and competence attracts the eye of her employer. By the end of the novel, he has proposed to her and they are preparing to live happily ever after—now that she has given up her "foolish" modern ways.

Other Norris heroines' youthful indiscretions are more difficult to live down. In *Harriet and the Piper* (1920), Harriet Field is mesmerized by the unscrupulous Royal Blondin when she is seventeen, and she enters into a brief secret marriage with him. Even though she later realizes "[t]here had been no marriage, of course, either in law or in fact" (295), the incident still haunts the heroine ten years later and almost wrecks her chances for future happiness. Even more disastrous is young Julia Page's youthful affair with an importunate suitor in *The Story of Julia Page* (1929). She feels obliged to confess her transgression to Jim Studdiford when he asks her to marry him. Although Studdiford maintains that he loves her anyway, his knowledge of her past sours their marriage. Julia eventually comes to understand that she can never expect happiness: she "knew now that life to her must be a battle; whatever the years to come might hold for her, they could not hold more than an occasional heavenly interval of peace." (418)

Kathleen Norris and Temple Bailey were both in their forties in the 1920s and Gene Stratton-Porter was in her fifties. They were scarcely flappers themselves. Perhaps we must turn to younger writers to find wholehearted acceptance of sexually liberated behavior for young women. Vina Delmar's first novel *Bad Girl* was published in 1928 when Delmar was twenty-three. The book achieved unexpected success, ranking fifth among best-selling fiction for the year. The following year, Delmar published another novel, *Kept Woman*, and a collection of short stories entitled *Loose Ladies*. Delmar's heroines appear at first glance to have shed traditional mores once and for all. The very model of modern flappers, they behave in a manner calculated to shock their elders. Delmar's young typists, salesclerks, and housewives bob their hair, rouge their lips, and roll their stockings above their knees. They smoke; they drink; they cross their legs in public. They are practiced at the quick comeback, at brittle repartee. When Eddie, for instance, first meets Dot in *Bad Girl*, he asks, "What about it? . . . Want to see me again?" Dot promptly retorts, "I should say not, but accidents do happen." (15)

The young women in Vina Delmar's stories and novels are more casual about sex than Stratton-Porter's, Bailey's, or Norris' heroines could ever be. They think nothing of kissing a young man on the first date. They are not adverse to petting, but for Delmar's characters, as for the young female population in general during this period, petting stops short of sexual intercourse.[8] Soon after encountering her on board a Hudson River excursion boat, Eddie considers his chances with Dot in *Bad Girl*. Based, apparently, upon previous experience with young women of Dot's presumed type, he predicts to himself that

she would move with him into a darkened corner and permit him to kiss her, to paw her unrestrainedly. The limit? No, she would not go the limit. She would lie against his shoulder, moist-lipped, panting, but ever alert lest the purely physical barrier that guaranteed her self-respect be taken away from her. (7)

One fails in the attempt to imagine the suitors of virginal Linda Strong or Jane Barnes entertaining such calculations. In Dot's case, she eventually surpasses Eddie's expectations: she goes "the limit." Immediately afterward Dot is ashamed of herself and Eddie is unable to reassure her.

"I wish everybody didn't think it was wrong," said Dot, very low.
"I guess other people have wished that." He sighed heavily.
"Don't you suppose," Dot asked, "that somewhere there are nice people who would think it was all right?"
"Maybe in France," Eddie replied, doubtfully. "Even the high-toned people over there are kind of loose, I've heard."
"Gee, Eddie, I'll feel awful down at work. I bet the girls will be able to tell right off that I've gone bad." (56)

For the young woman in a Delmar novel, then, even one sexual indiscretion threatens to ruin her reputation: she fears that her family, her friends, and her coworkers will all repudiate her. Only if her partner in scandal offers to marry her, as Eddie does in *Bad Girl*, can she regain her good name. (The young man involved, it goes without saying, is not sullied by the experience; the double standard is intact in the world of Delmar's characters—and, presumably, of Delmar's readers.) Dot quits her job and settles down contentedly to a life of domestic bliss.

Until she gets pregnant. Dot fears that Eddie will not want a child so, when she breaks the news to him, she is "careless and hard in the telling." (103) Eddie therefore believes that she does not want the baby. Dot and Eddie spend the next nine months deceiving one another. Each secretly wants the baby but is unable to admit it to the other. Dot, desperately eager to please Eddie, shrinks from acknowledging that she looks forward to something that he is apparently against. Eddie, habitually inarticulate and fearful for Dot's health during childbirth, cannot erase her misconceptions of his true feelings. It is not until they are on their way home from the hospital after the baby is born that Dot finally realizes Eddie cares deeply for the child. Dot is now free to admit her own pleasure at being a mother. Thus, Delmar's heroines may shock their elders by their clothing, their cigarettes, their rouged lips; they may affect the "hard-boiled" wit of their generation; they may even transgress the sexual mores of their age. But, beneath their jazz age exteriors, they cling to the old-fashioned values of marriage and motherhood—just like Stratton-Porter's and Bailey's heroines.

The "New Woman" who appears in *Bad Girl*—and in most other popular novels written by women in the Twenties—is somewhat different from the heroines featured by Scott Fitzgerald, the most influential interpreter of the flapper— a creature whom he described as "lovely, expensive—and about nineteen." (Quoted in Leuchtenburg 1958, 172) Unlike Daisy Buchannan, who lives for the moment, has become cynical about marriage, and contemplates an affair with Jay Gatsby, the women who most frequently people best-selling novels by female writers are seldom as liberated as we might have expected. In novel after novel, the protagonist is a woman who has adopted the veneer of flapperdom: the clothing, hairstyle, slang of the times; but who remains an old-fashioned girl at heart. This is consistent with the message presented in films of the period. As Sumiko Higashi observes in her study of the American silent movie heroine, "if women rebelled by behaving like rather than opposite men, their unconventional actions led to a conventional end. The flapper may have been sexually precocious but in fact, she was not really so distant from the sentimental heroine in terms of her goal": marriage to a physically attractive and economically dependable young man. (1978, 112) Even the apparent "sexual precociousness" of the movie heroine was restricted. Based upon her analysis of women's images in movies of the Twenties, Mary P. Ryan concludes that "[i]t would be very difficult . . . for a movie-going girl to receive the idea that sexual promiscuity was an approved form of behavior in the nineteen-twenties. The movie heroine was always chaste at heart. . . . Sex in the films of the twenties . . . heightened sexual awareness without promising ultimate gratification." (1976, 373) Likewise, movie historian Molly Haskell remarks that the "American [movie] flapper was, by definition, only superficially uninhibited. She was, after all, the middle-class . . . daughter of puritans, and she would pass this heritage on to her own daughters and granddaughters." (1974, 79)

Judge Ben Lindsay, best known for his advocacy of the notion of "companionate," or trial, marriage, predicted that "in a few years the lively flapper would become 'a happy, loyal wife with several children.' " (Quoted in Freedman 1974, 377) Popular women's fiction of the Twenties simultaneously substantiates and refutes Lindsay's assertion. In at least a few popular novels of the period, the heroines cast off traditional middle-class inhibitions to assert themselves more boldly than women had heretofore dared to do. Although most of these novels end with the heroines' marriage (or remarriage, in the case of *Ex-Wife*), one ventures to predict that these heroines will be as likely to exhibit their independence and their frank pleasure in sex after they are wed as they did before. In the majority of women's novels of the Twenties, however, the protagonists are more restrained. For Delmar's Dot Haley or Norris' Pamela Raleigh, being a flapper seemed to be only a matter of going through a "phase," negotiating a brief period of life between childhood and adulthood when a young woman was at liberty to act out a rebellion against traditional values which she in fact never really abandoned. Once she had taken on her "real" role as wife and mother, she cast aside all pretense of insurrection and settled down to a life of domesticity. Temple Bailey's or Gene Stratton-Porter's heroines, moreover, assume few of the mannerisms or behaviors commonly associated with the flapper; far from being intent on having a good time while they are young and single, their objective is to marry "Mr. Right," settle in a house in the country or the suburbs, and start a family.

The very fact that popular women novelists of the decade offered readers a Diana Mayo or a Lorelei Lee at the same time that they offered a Pamela Raleigh or a Jane Barnes suggests an ambivalence among women of the day as to the behavior and values they deemed appropriate for themselves. That the popular novelists of the day did not speak with one voice demonstrates that at least some of the traditional expectations for women were being renegotiated. In particular, a new morality was being established: women were coming to see themselves as sexual beings, with desires which were no longer to be repressed—after marriage, at least. Women were also coming to expect more emotional satisfaction from marriage, to look for a mate who would treat them as a partner, not as a subordinate. When it came to abandoning the cult of domesticity altogether, however, most Twenties couples were unprepared to take so drastic a step. As we shall see in the next chapter, women fully expected and wanted to be wives and mothers, to devote their undivided attention to the full-time occupation of homemaker. If the popular novels written by women for women in the Twenties are any indication, an era widely touted as one of sweeping social transformation produced only modest changes for most middle-class young women.

CHAPTER TWO

Married Women

Just as the Twenties was a period in which the nature and expectations of the young single woman were being renegotiated, so too was the Twenties an era in which the institution of marriage was changing in character. Again, the shift in public perception, this time of marriage, was reflected in popular women's novels of the day. Just as we have seen to be the case with the depiction of young unmarried women, so too with the portrayal of marriage: the fact that a few writers formulated a relatively "modern" picture of marriage should not blind us from seeing that the majority of best-selling women novelists conceived of marital relationships in more traditional terms.

The popular woman writer whose novels most consistently and forcefully portray a more modern conception of marriage was Dorothy Canfield Fisher. Canfield, who used her maiden name for her fiction and her married name for her nonfiction, was born in Kansas in 1879. Her father began his working life as a college professor and later became president of a succession of Midwestern state universities; her mother was an artist who had studied painting in Paris. Canfield was hardly "only" a novelist: she completed a doctorate in Romance languages at Columbia University in 1904, could speak at least six foreign languages, was the first woman appointed to the Vermont state board of education, and was a member of the first board of selection of the Book-of-the-Month Club, remaining the only woman on the board for twenty-five years. She published her first novel and married Columbia graduate John Redfield Fisher in 1907, and the couple settled in Vermont, where they raised two children. A full-time writer, Canfield turned out a steady stream of articles and short stories, and she published eleven novels in the course of her career, two of which, *The*

Brimming Cup and *The Home-Maker*, appeared on the best-seller lists for 1921 and 1924, respectively.[1]

In her second published novel *The Squirrel-Cage* (1912) Canfield called for readers to embrace the central concepts of what would, a decade later, be called "companionate marriage." Companionate marriage, according to social historians Steven Mintz and Susan Kellogg's definition, was to be a new kind of marriage, a union "held together not by rigid social pressures or religious conceptions of moral duty but by mutual affection, sexual attraction, and equal rights." (1988, 115) The novel's protagonist Lydia Emery is emotionally and intellectually drawn to Daniel Rankin who, having decided that there are things in life more important than making money and getting ahead, has abandoned his business career to live in the woods and earn his living as a carpenter. Rankin, who presumably speaks for the author, believes that marriage should be a relationship based upon "sure-enough shared interests." He criticizes the average middle-class couple, claiming that the husband "doesn't want to bother with children, or with the servant problem or the questions of family life, and he doesn't want his wife bothering him in his business any more than she wants him interfering with hers." (1912, 107–8) Despite her attraction to Rankin and his ideas, Lydia is pressured by her family into marrying Paul Hollister, an ambitious young businessman whose expectations concerning marriage are as traditional as Rankin's are progressive.

Once married, Paul and Lydia's life settles into the pattern Rankin has railed against. Lydia soon becomes dissatisfied with "her remoteness from her husband's world" (257) and makes "tentative efforts to construct a bridge between her world and his," (253) efforts which Paul continually repulses. When Lydia, for example, tries to convince her husband that they should "live together a little more, to have a few more thoughts in common" (300), Paul angrily retorts that "what *I* think is that if my dear young wife would spend more time looking after her own business she'd have fewer complaints to make about my doing the same. The thing for you to do is to accept conditions as they are and do your best in them—and, really, Lydia, make your best a little better." (303)

Although Lydia remains hopeful that she will eventually prevail upon Paul to help her restructure their marriage, the reader suspects that Lydia will never succeed. Given the incompatibility of Lydia's and Paul's conceptions of marriage, Canfield seems to have felt that she had no choice but to kill off Paul in an industrial accident. Shocked by her husband's sudden death and close to term in her second pregnancy, Lydia is irrationally afraid that she will die in childbirth and that her children will be brought up by relatives who share Paul's philosophy of life. To forestall such a prospect, she asks Daniel Rankin to adopt her children. Fortunately, Lydia pulls through, and the reader assumes that she will marry Rankin and finally start living as she would like—as an equal partner in a marriage in which both spouses fully share their lives together.

In *The Squirrel-Cage*, although the husband is encouraged to take an active role in childrearing and the wife is urged to familiarize herself with her husband's business activities, even to help with his work from time to time, each spouse still retains primary responsibility for his or her respective sphere of activity. The emphasis is upon sharing marital duties, not upon exchanging them. In *The Home-Maker* (1924), published over a decade after *The Squirrel-Cage* appeared in print, Canfield goes a bit further. She presents a husband and wife who do indeed swap roles. At the beginning of the novel, Canfield introduces us to two characters who are completely unsuited for the marital responsibilities society expects them to perform. Evangeline Knapp undertakes her domestic chores competently but grimly. In her heart she knows she hates housework. As for her children, she has "passionate love and devotion to give them, but neither patience nor understanding." (1924, 307) The community may admire her immaculate house, her neat and well-mannered children and conclude she is an outstanding example of the "complacent unquestioned generalization, 'The mother is the natural home-maker.' " (307) Yet, her husband Lester finally admits to himself,

what a juggernaut it had been in their case! How poor Eva, drugged by the cries of its devotees, had cast herself down under its grinding wheels—and had dragged the children in under with her. It wasn't because Eva had not tried her best. She had nearly killed herself trying. But she had been like a gifted mathematician set to paint a picture. (307–8)

Lester is equally unfit for his role as family breadwinner. Lester hates business as much as Evangeline loathes domesticity. Knowing that the community considers him a failure, Lester feels guilty that he cannot muster enough enthusiasm and aggressiveness to win a promotion, that he cannot even keep his mind on his work steadily enough to avoid reprimands from his immediate superiors. Matters come to a crisis when Lester is fired from his job. Before he has had time to give Evangeline the bad news, Lester has an accident which leaves him an invalid. As in *The Squirrel-Cage*, Canfield pushes her characters in *The Home-Maker* into changing their lives by subjecting them to forces beyond their control. Because of Lester's fall, Evangeline must become the breadwinner of the family, and Lester must shoulder the responsibilities of the homemaker.

It quickly becomes clear to the reader that Evangeline and Lester are now performing the tasks for which they are best suited. A born businesswoman, Eva is happy for the first time since her marriage. With her positive attitude, good business head, and flair for fashion, Evangeline is a success, soon earning a much higher salary than Lester had ever commanded. Meanwhile, Lester finds that he is an adequate housekeeper and an excellent parent. The "natural, right human thing to do," Lester realizes to himself, is "to stay at home and make the home, since a home-maker was needed." (308)

Eva and Lester are not aggressive standard-bearers for the cause of feminism; at the beginning of the novel, they accept their socially-sanctioned roles without question. They exchange places only when they are forced to do so by circumstance, when Lester becomes physically incapable of being a wage earner. If Lester's condition should improve, they are prepared, albeit reluctantly, to resume their "normal" responsibilities. Fortunately for the Knapp family, the family doctor steps in to ensure that Eva and Lester will maintain the roles for which they are most competent. Though Dr. Merritt is well aware that Lester is close to complete recovery, he cautions Eva that her husband should never try to use his legs again, that it might even be fatal to do so. While the modern reader might suspect the author has chosen Lester's specific injury to suggest that he has become emasculated, that he is to be pitied for having lost his masculine prerogative to act as breadwinner and head of the household, Canfield provides no evidence for this interpretation. Instead, the novel ends with the Knapp children assuring one another with great relief that their father will never be cured, and one is left with the assumption that all of the members of the Knapp family will live happily ever after.

In *The Home-Maker*, Canfield is not so much advocating sweeping changes in the roles of married men and women as encouraging her readers to be more receptive to the idea that husbands and wives should choose for themselves the tasks which they can do best; she is urging her readers to be accepting of those couples who conclude that the traditional marital roles are not right for them. As she wrote in a *Los Angeles Examiner* article published the same year that *The Home-Maker* appeared, "We could realize that every human being is different from every other, and hence each couple of human beings is different from every other couple; and, within the limits of possibility and decency we could leave people free to construct the sort of marriage that is best for their particular combination." (Canfield 1924, vi)

In *The Squirrel-Cage* and *The Home-Maker* Canfield explicitly counsels her readers to question conventional marital roles, to share and—if it seems right for them—even to exchange traditional responsibilities. In these novels Canfield also implicitly urges her readers to construct marriages free from the restraints of patriarchal authority. Certainly, neither Daniel Rankin nor Lester Knapp attempt to dominate their wives nor to make family decisions unilaterally. In *The Brimming Cup* (1921) Canfield foregrounds this issue by portraying a marriage in which the husband consciously refrains from attempting to exert control over his wife, even though his lack of intervention may cost him his marriage. After several years of marriage, Marise Crittenden is beginning to feel vaguely bored. The last of her three children has just started school and, quite suddenly, there is no one claiming her constant attention. Marise still loves her husband Neale, but the physical excitement has faded from their relationship. For the first time, Marise feels that she is middle-aged, that the tide in her life is "ebbing." (108) In this mood she is vulnerable to the attractions of the virile and cosmopolitan Vincent Marsh, who unexpectedly appears in the small Vermont village where the Crittendens live and who, Marise comes to believe, "could lift her from the dulled routine of life beginning to fade and lose its colors, and carry her back to the glorious forgetfulness of every created thing, save one man and one woman." (348) Marise appeals to her husband Neale to insist that she must stay with her family, but Neale has never before presumed to make her decisions for her and he refuses to do so now. Despite the pain it causes him, Neale leaves the choice up to Marise, telling her, "What I'm saying, what I'm always saying, dear, and trying my best to live, is that everybody must decide for himself when a general proposition applies to him, what to believe about his own life and its values. Nobody else can tell him." (234)

In a chapter entitled "Marise's Coming-of-Age," Marise struggles to do what Neale has advised, to try boldly to understand her life, to examine her alternatives, and to determine the course which is right for her to take. Eventually she realizes that "[i]f it had only been traditional morality, reproaching her with traditional complaints about the overstepping of traditional bounds," she would not hesitate to go off with Vincent Marsh. (351) But, she admits to herself, it is only "physical excitement" and "great ease of life" that Marsh can offer. (352) When she decides to reject Marsh's offer and to remain with Neale and her children, she feels liberated, not because she has made the conventionally correct choice but because, for the first time in her life, she has had the courage to set her own course. She finds that she is finally a "free woman, free from that something in her heart that was afraid. . . . Why, here was the total fulfillment she had longed for. Here was the life more abundant, within, within her own heart, waiting for her!" (358)

In their studies of popular literature, both Joan Shelley Rubin and Erik Lofroth view Canfield's repudiation of Victorian sexual mores in *The Brimming Cup* as a sign of modernity: according to Rubin, the novelist "established her modern credentials by facing sex squarely and refraining from conventional moralism." (1992, 128) However, Rubin and Lofroth are divided in their assessment of Canfield's emphasis upon the importance of acting according to the dictates of personal morality. While Rubin sees Canfield's espousal of the "necessity of faithfulness to an inner self" as the result of the fact that she "adhered, at base, to an older outlook," (1992, 128) Lofroth regards the writer's moral relativism as being as much a twentieth-century notion as are Canfield's views on sexuality. Lofroth remarks that Marise Crittenden "is confronted with a moral choice where no action is simply right or wrong, no alternative sacred, but only valid in relation to its time and place"—and in relation to the needs and desires of the individual making the choice. (1983, 182) Whether one reads Canfield's stress upon moral decision making as a sign of her modernity or as evidence of a continued faith in Emersonian self-reliance, there is no question that, for Dorothy Canfield, the process is of more significance than the outcome: the fact that Marise has had the strength to make her own decision is more important than the nature of the decision itself. Marise has gained self-awareness and insight through her struggle and, the author suggests, it is as a result of this inner conflict that she has achieved maturity. Now as certain of her values as is Neale himself, Marise is finally ready to enter into a truly "companionate" marriage, a union in which both partners are equally strong, in which both share in each other's lives, and in which both find emotional fulfillment and happiness.

A writer who displays an attitude toward marriage which is strikingly similar to that of Dorothy Canfield is Susan Glaspell. Although she is best known as a short-story writer and a playwright who, along with Eugene O'Neill, was one of the founders of the Provincetown Players, Glaspell also published several novels.[2] In *Ambrose Holt and Family* (1931) Harriette "Blossom" Holt's predicament is much like that of Lydia Hollister in Canfield's *The Squirrel-Cage*. Like Lydia, Harriette has married a man who will not take her seriously, a spouse who refuses to share his interests with his wife—a husband, that is, who is totally unlike Canfield's Daniel Rankin or Neale Crittenden. Harriette's husband persists in calling her "Blossom," a name which indicates that Lincoln Holt regards his wife as a child. Although dissatisfied with her situation, Harriette does not actively rebel until Lincoln's father arrives in town. Although Ambrose Holt remains only briefly upon the scene, his inclusion in the novel's title underscores his importance to the story. He serves as a catalyst for change in the attitudes and relationships of the other major characters. Harriette quickly becomes friends with him, partly because the older man treats Harriette as an adult and partly because he understands Harriette's feelings. Ambrose, too, has been stereotyped. He tells his daughter-in-law, "Well, you see they knew just who I was and they expected me to be just that, and that is a little as if they were putting a pillow on my face and sitting on it." (104) Holt's solution was to leave town—and his family. Harriette decides to stand her ground and to become more assertive with her husband. Although the initial result is that Lincoln follows his father's example and disappears, Lincoln eventually returns and he and Harriette develop a deeper, more honest relationship. Lincoln may not have let go of "Blossom" altogether, but he can also accept Harriette. Harriette Holt does not appear to have achieved the equality and independence that Lydia Hollister Rankin can expect or that Marise Crittenden enjoys, but Harriette is satisfied with her partial victory: "It was all right. One took what was there, and went ahead." (315)[3]

In their treatment of the nature and purpose of marriage, Canfield and Glaspell are somewhat unique among best-selling women novelists of the time in their thoroughgoing reevaluation of the marital relationship. More common is the treatment of marriage offered by Kathleen Norris. As we have seen in the previous chapter, this writer reaffirms traditional expectations of married women just as she presents flappers who conform to conventional norms of behavior. While Canfield and Glaspell question the doctrine of separate spheres, the notion that wives should confine their activities to the domestic arena, Norris endorses the practice. Those Norris characters who do not meet this wifely code of conduct are deemed irresponsible, even wicked. Their failings serve to highlight those traits we are meant to admire in the married protagonists.

In *The Story of Julia Page* (1929), it is the heroine's own mother who provides the cautionary tale for the reader. Emeline Page is lazy and irresponsible. Norris tells us that her husband "thought she was a poor housekeeper, an extravagant shopper, a wretched cook, and worse than all, a sloven about her personal appearance" (12–13)—and it is clear that Norris shares this opinion. Page and her husband begin to drift apart. When their daughter Julia is not quite seven, the Pages are divorced. Although Norris has described both husband and wife as selfish, she places most of the blame for the breakup of the Pages' marriage upon Emeline. Norris comments:

Poor Emeline—she could easily have held him! A little tenderness toward him, a little interest in her home and her child, and George would have been won again. Had he but once come home to a contented wife and a clean house, George's wavering affection would have been regained. (28–29)

Above all, Donald Makosky observes in his study of the portrayal of women in magazine short stories, a wife must create an "atmosphere of warmth and casual comfort" in the family home. (1966, 194) It is clear that Norris subscribes to this point of view. Those women characters in her novels who do not meet this standard are censured by the author.

In contrast, most Norris heroines take naturally to domesticity. Pamela Raleigh in *The Foolish Virgin* (1929) brings order out of chaos as paid companion on Gregory Chard's ranch, and Chard promptly proposes marriage. In *Barberry Bush* (1929), Barbara Atherton struggles to keep house in the old-fashioned, run-down ranch to which her new husband brings her; despite her efforts, the ungrateful and self-centered Barry du Spain soon leaves her. In *Passion Flower* (1930), wealthy Cassy Pringle has never kept house before her elopement with Dan Wallace, the family chauffeur. With advice from her new neighbors and through trial and error, she learns to cook, to wash and iron, and to budget their meager income. Soon she has created a "speckless, orderly domain" (77) very different from the state of the other cheap apartments in her building—tended, Norris implies, by working-class housewives who have not been raised to value cleanliness as fervently as the middle-class Cassy.

In Norris' novels, so-called "Bad Women" are even worse mothers than they are housewives. Invariably, they do not welcome children and do all they can to avoid or terminate pregnancy. Failing to prevent the baby's birth, they show little interest in raising the child. In Kathleen Norris' *Rose of the World* (1924), Jack Talbot foolishly rejects heroine Rose Kirby, a beautiful girl on the verge of blossoming into a woman who will be "earnest, sweet, impressionable—above all, touchingly, almost alarmingly 'good.' " (37) Instead, Jack marries antiheroine Edith Rogers, whom he quickly discovers is "really a child, spoiled, egotistical, self-centered, superficial . . . and absolutely devoid of affection." (138–39) When Edith gets pregnant, she cares more for riding her horse than for protecting the health of her unborn child; she has a fall, suffers a miscarriage, and dies.

Villainesses may try to avoid bearing children in order to spend more time on themselves, but heroines with such an objective soon realize their mistake and come to welcome the opportunity to devote themselves to raising families. In an era in which the size of middle-class families was decidedly on the decline, Kathleen Norris urged her readers not to stint on the size of their families, to realize, in the words of the hero of *Mother* (1911), "there's something magnificent in a woman . . . who begins eight destinies instead of one!" (170) Most of Norris' heroines instinctively desire lots of children and even those, like the protagonist of *Mother*, who are inclined to limit their families quickly realize the error of their ways.

Although Temple Bailey's novels tend to focus upon courtship rather than marriage, it is obvious that she too holds predominately traditional attitudes toward marriage. Like Norris, Bailey reaffirms the cult of domesticity. In *Peacock Feathers* (1924), Mimi LeBrun was raised to expect others to wait upon her, like Norris' Cassy Pringle. Unlike Cassy, Mimi does not adjust easily to keeping house for the man she loves. When Mimi marries Jerry Chandler and settles on his uncle's ranch out West, she is bitterly disappointed to discover that her new home is not the luxurious estate she had anticipated. Chandler tries to enable his new wife to continue to live in the style to which she is accustomed—by shouldering the domestic responsibilities himself. He does not realize that Mimi's standards are slowly changing, that she is becoming ready to abandon her social pretensions and become a "proper" wife by taking on her duties as a full-time homemaker. Once Mimi does so, the tensions between husband and wife dissolve, and it is clear that they will live happily ever after.

Most of Bailey's other heroines are domestic by nature. In *Wallflowers* (1927), Sandra Claybourne happily and competently keeps house for her mother and sister. On a typical morning, Sandra "washed the dishes, straightened the rooms, changed her dress, and a little after eleven went out on the balcony with her book and a basket of sewing." (45) An equally good housewife, Jane Barnes in *The Dim Lantern* (1923) keeps her brother's house as neat as she keeps herself: "In winter everything was burnished and bright; in summer crisp curtains waved in the warm breeze; there were cool shadows within the clean, quiet rooms." (135) It does not take long for Sandra's and Jane's domestic virtues to be recognized by eligible bachelors, who propose marriage before the end of the novels.

Bailey's heroines are equally willing to assume the responsibilities of motherhood, although in general it is the heroes who first dream of children, not the heroines. In *The Blue Window* (1926), Crispin purchases the dwelling he hopes to share with Hildegarde even before she has accepted his hand in marriage. He moves into the house, seeing his beloved "in every room, but most often by the fireplace. . . . And far away in the future . . . around the hearth . . . a small and shining troop . . . flitting back and forth in the firelight." (313) Likewise, in *The Dim Lantern* (1923) Evans Follette dreams of a little house in which Jane Barnes will live as his wife. He dreams of a "living-room where a fire burned bright . . . [and a] kitchen, a shining place, with a crisp maid to save Jane from drudgery. Two crisp maids, perhaps, some day, if there were kiddies." (203) One assumes that the heroes' dreams are, in fact, Bailey's own, that the author has projected her idea of the perfect marriage—complete with "crisp maids"—into the thoughts of her principal male characters. It is a feminine picture of domestic bliss which is articulated by the leading men—and quickly embraced by the heroines themselves.

The emphasis upon hearth and home in Bailey's novels underscores her conception of the ideal wife in terms of the cult of domesticity. Suitor after suitor follows Crispin's example in imagining his sweetheart beside the fireplace in a little house in the country. Bailey's heroines, moreover, share their lovers' dreams. We know that Sally Hulbert in *The Blue Window* is not the flighty girl she appears on the surface when she admits that "underneath I want to wear [old-fashioned] caps and part my hair and warm my toes at the fire." (1926, 113) In *Wallflowers*, Sandra Claybourne initially conceives of her relationship with Rufus Fiske in terms of romance, not domesticity. She tells him: "At first, I didn't think of hearthstones, Rufus. I thought of gardens and secret stairs and Romeo and Aucassin." But eventually Rufus' vision replaces her own. She confesses that "now . . . it is the thought that I'm your wife . . . that I shall sit by your fire" (1927, 350) that is her deepest desire.

Despite her emphasis upon the traditional notion of domesticity, Temple Bailey reflects a relatively modern conception of wedlock in some respects: in her novels, as in Canfield's, husband and wife are companions, and the goal of marriage appears to be the achievement of mutual happiness. The man that the Bailey heroine marries is above all a friend. He is a person with whom the protagonist is comfortable and in whom she can confide. In *Silver Slippers* (1928), Giles Armiger falls in love with Joan Dudley at first sight. But it is more than romance which draws them together; it is also the fact that they share the same values, have the same interests. It takes Joan longer to realize that she is in love with Giles, as she is infatuated with the handsome but weak Drew Hallam, who is too shallow and self-centered to make her a compatible husband. Giles never loses hope that he will ultimately gain Joan's hand. His greatest desire is to "share his dreams with Joan, to have her by his side, his precious companion, his perfect comrade!" (350) In *Little Girl Lost* (1932), Araminta Williams discovers that what she wants in marriage is not to be worshipped as a saint on a pedestal but to be loved as a woman of flesh and blood. Wifehood, she tells one suitor, "means having common interests—in meeting you at the door at night, and saying 'good-bye' in the morning. It means all the deep and sacred things of life, and it means, too, all the friendly and pleasant ones." (185)

In most of Bailey's novels, as in the Harlequin Romances of the postwar era, the heroine at first falls in love with the wrong man, a suitor who is not worthy of the heroine and will not make her a good husband. It is only when the heroine finally sees this beau in his true light—and realizes that it is the hero waiting in the wings who is the "right" man for her—that the novel can draw to a close. Because Bailey focuses so exclusively on the heroine's search for the perfect husband, her novels delineate in some detail the traits this paragon should possess, and the author dwells at length upon the characteristics of the marital relationship which both heroine and hero hope to achieve. Norris' novels do not follow as rigid a formula as do Bailey's. Norris seems more interested in fashioning contrived, complicated plots than in ensuring her heroines' ultimate marital happiness. While Norris, albeit less consistently than Bailey, implies that spouses should be companions who share common goals and attitudes, she is more likely to depict heroines who are doggedly faithful to undeserving husbands or who are kept apart by circumstance from more praiseworthy suitors than to reward her protagonists with compatible—and emotionally nurturing—mates.

Despite the strong emphasis upon emotional congeniality in Bailey's novels and the weaker stress upon it in Norris' books, these two writers' notion of "companionate" marriage is quite different from Canfield's or Glaspell's. While Canfield and Glaspell question the traditional doctrine of separate spheres, Bailey and Norris reinforce it. In their novels, as in the majority of popular works of fiction of the era, the woman is expected to care for her husband and their children and to manage the household in exchange for her spouse's financial support and protection. As Nancy F. Cott observes in *The Grounding of Modern Feminism*, "[i]ncorporating sex and marital camaraderie, yet leaving intact the sexual division of labor, the companionate model was broadcast far afield of the Feminist camp by a range of spokesmen and women." (1987, 157) Best-selling women novelists of the era tended to fall into the popularizers' ranks. While E. M. Hull and

Anita Loos acknowledged women's sexual drives, Temple Bailey and Kathleen Norris focused upon the emotional intimacy to be achieved through marriage. Almost ignored, except perhaps in the fiction of Dorothy Canfield, Susan Glaspell, and, as we shall see, Edith Wharton, was the feminists' indictment of the gender inequalities inherent in middle-class marriage.

In a discussion of American women novelists' treatment of marriage, it is impossible to ignore the work of Edith Wharton, our most celebrated early-twentieth-century woman author and a writer whose novels and short stories repeatedly focus on issues of marriage and divorce. While Wharton is universally regarded as a "serious" author whose subtlety and style are much admired by literary scholars, she can be considered a popular novelist as well. *The House of Mirth* (1905), *The Age of Innocence* (1920), and *Twilight Sleep* (1927) were all best sellers. Although in the first two decades of the century Wharton's stories, poems, articles, and novels appeared only in the relatively highbrow *Scribner's Magazine* and *The Atlantic*, by the Twenties and Thirties the author was a frequent contributor to the more middlebrow "picture" publications, such as *Woman's Home Companion, Ladies' Home Journal, Saturday Evening Post*, and *The Delineator*.[4]

If one posits that popular writers tend to reflect mainstream American values and aspirations in their fiction, one must acknowledge certain difficulties in applying this premise to Edith Wharton and her works, especially with regard to her novels of the Twenties and Thirties. By the mid-Twenties, as Wharton scholar Cynthia Griffin Wolff remarks, "[c]hanges were taking place everywhere; her [Wharton's] generation was being supplanted. . . . More important, she was growing dangerously out of touch with the world that she felt forevermore to be *her* world—American society, the society of fashionable New York especially." 1977, 373) Wolff's observation touches upon several factors which distanced Wharton from contemporary middle-class American thought. Firstly, Wharton was in her sixties and seventies during these decades; her views had been shaped by an earlier era. Secondly, Wharton may have continued to be an American citizen, but she had not lived in the United States for any length of time since well before the Great War broke out in Europe; she could not claim to be speaking for a people with whom she no longer had daily contact. While Wharton herself was sensitive to criticism that she had lost the American "idiom" and tentatively planned a visit to the United States for a "fresh examination of the language and customs of the people she so tenaciously thought of as her own," (373) her first trip to America in over a decade was an eleven-day stay in 1923; she made no more voyages to her native land before her death in 1934. Thirdly, Wharton's upper-class position largely insulated her from the lives of middle-class Americans. Her social, cultural, and intellectual interests were hardly those of the average American woman. Her life-style had little in common with that of the typical middle-class woman, either. In an era in which seventy-one percent of all American families earned less than $2,500 a year (McElvaine 1984, 38), Wharton's income was higher, to say the least. As Wharton biographer R.W.B. Lewis reports, "[o]ver the period from 1920 through 1924, it would be fair to estimate that her work brought in about $250,000. This was on top of an average annual private income of some $30,000." (1975, 459)

Wharton's writing itself poses a problem for the cultural historian. When attempting to uncover the social values of a writer with Edith Wharton's sensibility one must pick one's way carefully. Her tone is often one of detached irony, and her personal views are frequently hard to tease out of her writings. Wharton keeps her distance from her characters more than most popular novelists; viewpoints expressed by her protagonists frequently do not reflect her own perspective. Furthermore, the author often depicts the mores and values of the past; the reader is left to determine the extent to which Wharton believes these attitudes and behaviors still pertain to the world of the present.

Despite these impediments to interpretation, we can venture to make some observations regarding Wharton's positions regarding marriage and divorce, although Wharton scholars are somewhat divided in their assessment of the author's constancy of outlook over time. In *After the Vows Were Spoken: Marriage in American Literary Realism* (1984), Allen F. Stein claims that there is "no change over the years in Wharton's attitude toward marriage" (218), that Wharton consistently thought of "marriage as invariably imperfect but invariably of potential value." (210) On the other hand, Elizabeth Ammons, in *Edith Wharton's Argument with America* (1980), maintains that there is a "drastic" change in Wharton's "argument" beginning in the early Twenties, when "she moves from a liberal to a conservative position on the 'woman question.' " (160) "Whereas she formerly sympathized with aspirant women trapped by marriage and the lack of desirable alternatives," Ammons asserts, Wharton "now argues that marriage and domestic life are woman's best means of self-fulfillment." (165) My reading of Wharton's work suggests that there is a shift in her treatment of marriage over the years but that it is more subtle than Ammons maintains. I am inclined to agree with Cynthia Griffin Wolff, whose interpretation of Wharton's fiction seems to indicate that, even though the tone and focus of her work changed considerably over the years as Wharton's emotional life unfolded and as the author's perspective shifted with age, Wharton's basic values remained relatively stable.

Up until the mid-teens, Wharton repeatedly concentrates on depicting marriage as a trap in which it is usually the wife who is imprisoned, a perspective closer to that of Dorothy Canfield and Susan Glaspell than to that of Kathleen Norris and Temple Bailey. However, while Canfield and Glaspell permit their protagonists to free themselves from their confinement, to achieve more equitable marital relationships with their spouses,

Wharton allows her characters no release. Given the difficulties of Wharton's relationship during these years with her own husband, one assumes that she is rehearsing her own predicament. In "The Other Two" (1904), Wharton presents marriage as an institution which effectively suppresses a woman's individuality and freedom. The story is told from the point of view of the husband, who has recently married a woman twice divorced. While Waythorn is at first pleased with Alice, whose "composure was restful to him" (380), as Waythorn and his wife are thrown into association with Alice's two earlier husbands he comes to view his wife's adaptability in a different light. "Her elasticity," Waythorn concludes, "was the result of tension in too many different directions." (393) "The Other Two" might be read as a criticism of the effects of divorce; more to the point, it is a criticism of marriage. It questions a social standard which expects a woman to bend her will to that of her husband. The result of such a process has irrevocably harmed the protagonist's wife, who is the true subject of this story: "Alice Haskett—Alice Varick—Alice Waythorn—she had been each in turn, and had left hanging to each name a little of her privacy, a little of her personality, a little of the inmost self where the unknown god abides." (393) Alice Waythorn has encountered none of the violence or cruelty which subdues Minnie Foster's spirit in Glaspell's "Trifles" (1916) (see note 3), but no less decisively she has been forced to relinquish her individuality upon marriage.

In *The House of Mirth* (1905), Lily Bart escapes marital imprisonment and the repression, even erasure, of her personality—but at tremendous cost. A "victim of the civilization which had produced her" (7), Lily has no way to satisfy her craving for luxury save by marrying a wealthy man. Again and again, Lily comes close to capturing an eligible prey, only to draw back at the last minute. It is not the institution of marriage itself, however, which Wharton seems to be criticizing in this novel, but marriage as it exists in upper-class American society. Although *The House of Mirth* is filled with images of unsatisfactory matrimony, highlighted by the marriages of the Trenors, Lily, who speaks for Wharton herself, seems to have an ideal notion of marriage against which all of her prospects are found wanting. And Wharton does present one "perfect" marriage: working-class Nettie Crane's union with George Struther. Nettie, whom Lily had once helped in a time of need, tells Lily that she had been in more trouble than Lily had known. She had had an affair with a "gentleman" who promised to marry her, then he had left her. When George Struther proposed to Nettie, she had told him everything. "George cared for me enough," Nettie tells Lily, "to have me as I was" (315), and Nettie is able to make a fresh start in life. Later that night, before Lily takes the fatal dose of sleeping drops, she compares Nettie's situation to her own. "Lily remembered Nettie's words: *I knew he knew about me.* Her husband's faith in her had made her renewal possible—it is so easy for a woman to become what the man she loves believes her to be! Well—Selden had twice been ready to stake his faith on Lily Bart; but the third trial had been too severe for his endurance." (320) The tragedy in *House of Mirth* lies in the fact that neither Lily nor Lawrence Selden has the courage to follow their instincts and join together in a "republic of the spirit." (68) Lily's sense that marriage should be something more than a financial arrangement stops her from marrying Gryce or Rosedale; her inability to renounce wealth and comfort prevents her from trying another means of achieving happiness—through marriage to Selden—just as Selden's failure to "transcend the codes of his class and place" makes it equally impossible for him to accept Lily unconditionally, as George Struther has accepted Nettie Crane. (Olin-Ammentorp 1988, 240)[5]

Unlike Lily Bart, Undine Spragg in *The Custom of the Country* (1913), "accepts the commercial nature of matrimony and is willing to negotiate herself on the marriage market." (Ammons, 98) Undine masters the business of matrimony just as her father and Elmer Moffatt manipulate the world of finance. Undine's misfortune is that she can never operate in the arena occupied by Abner Spragg and Moffatt. Her sex prevents her from applying her ferocious energy, cunning, and ambition to the "real business of life." (Wharton 1913, 209) With the will and initiative to succeed on Wall Street, Undine's native ability is distorted to fit within the boundaries of the drawing room and she becomes a "monstrously perfect result of the system" which forces men and women to occupy separate spheres. (208)

Like Dorothy Canfield and Susan Glaspell, Edith Wharton is questioning the notion that women must devote themselves solely to domestic concerns, that wives and daughter are to remain ignorant of all that transpires in the office. However, while Lydia Hollister in *The Squirrel-Cage* and Evangeline Knapp in *The Home-Maker* are unhappy victims of the cult of domesticity, until events alleviate their suffering, Undine Spragg is not so passive. She successfully manipulates the institution of marriage as she finds it. On the other hand, her second husband Ralph Marvell strives to realize an ideal conception of marriage. Thus, Wharton again reaffirms the potential inherent in marriage even as she depicts marriages that are far from perfect. As Stein notes, "despite the dearth of good marriages in this work . . . *The Custom of the Country*, like Wharton's other depictions of marital difficulties, constitutes no attack on matrimony. Implicit in her bitter, melodramatic account of Ralph's marriage is a defense of the relationship that Undine scorns." (1984, 244) Wharton's sympathetic treatment of Ralph moves the reader to feel compassion for the young man whose illusions are shattered and whose hopes are blighted by his ruthless and self-centered wife. In Dorothy Canfield's novels, her protagonists escape from the coils of "marriage as usual" to achieve fulfilling relationships with their spouses; Edith Wharton's fictional worlds of the early twentieth century are governed by a darker vision: Wharton's characters may long for marriages based upon companionship and love, but they are seldom able to achieve them.

By the 1920s, Edith Wharton began to suggest that mutually satisfying marriages were not unattainable visions but were within the grasp of her protagonists. Although Newland Archer in *The Age of Innocence* (1920), a novel which will be discussed more fully in a later chapter, is forced to renounce the woman he loves for the sake of the woman he marries, he realizes years later that his marriage has been a sound one. His encounter with Ellen Olenska changed him, in the words of Louis Auchincloss, "from a stuffed shirt into a man." (1962, ix) Archer has matured into a responsible, mature individual who "can contemplate that process [of distancing himself from Ellen] with a reflective, poignant sense of an irrecoverable loss that has in the end been overbalanced by the value of what has been saved." (Wolff 1977, 329) Ever since he abandoned the notion of eloping with Ellen, Archer has been a faithful husband and a good father. He may not have attained the ideal marriage, but he has acquitted his matrimonial duties well.

Perhaps the most "perfect" marriage in an Edith Wharton novel is that which Susy and Nick Lansing are on the brink of achieving at the end of *The Glimpses of the Moon* (1922). At the beginning of the novel both are relatively impoverished hangers-on in the world of the wealthy who are attracted to each other but believe that marriage to one another is impractical. Nevertheless, although Susy had planned to "wait till she found some one who combined the maximum of wealth with at least a minimum of companionableness" (7), she concocts a scheme whereby she and Nick can marry temporarily while they wait for better prospects to come along. Nick agrees, and they embark upon the first of a series of projected honeymoons in various homes lent to them by their wealthy friends. Within months, Nick leaves in a huff, angry at discovering that Susy's ethical standards are apparently more elastic than his own. More months pass. Although they come close to divorce, the two are finally reconciled. They realize that the marriage they entered into as a temporary union has become a permanent relationship. As Susy says to Nick, "The point is that we're *married*. . . . Married. . . . Doesn't it mean something to you, something—inexorable? It does to me. I didn't dream it would—in just that way." (348) Nick agrees. "He and she belonged to each other for always: he understood that now. The impulse which had first drawn them together again, in spite of reason, in spite of themselves almost, that deep-seated instinctive need that each had of the other, would never again wholly let them go." (363) While Wolff remarks of *The Glimpses of the Moon* that "perhaps nothing reveals its fundamental flaws more directly than the pat, sentimental denouement" (1977, 347) which is more characteristic of a Kathleen Norris best seller than a Wharton novel, the book's literary failings should not blind us to the author's message. In this reworking of Lily Bart's story, heroine and hero are able to join together in Selden's "republic of the spirit." Marriage need not be a prison for husband or wife. Wharton may have changed her emphasis since she wrote *The House of Mirth* nearly twenty years earlier, but her basic attitude toward marriage has remained unchanged: no matter how many imperfect unions may exist, perfect ones are possible as well. While only the secondary characters are able to achieve an ideal marriage in *The House of Mirth*, in *The Glimpses of the Moon* it is the main characters who do so.

Despite the fact that Edith Wharton is vastly more accomplished a writer than most of the other best-selling women novelists we have discussed in this chapter, her conception of marriage is not so different from theirs. For Wharton, as for the majority of popular women writers of her day, marital responsibilities are well defined. The wife is the caretaker; the husband, the breadwinner. While this conception of the division of labor is little changed from nineteenth-century notions of middle-class marriage, to focus only on attitudes regarding the allocation of matrimonial spheres of influence is to miss the profound shift which had taken place in middle-class expectations toward marriage since the late nineteenth century. In nearly all of the novels we have examined here, the emphasis is no longer upon the Victorian notion of duty but upon a more modern conception of self-fulfillment. Nineteenth-century women were expected to be satisfied if their marriage provided them with material security; as the best-selling women's novels of the early twentieth century indicate, middle-class women were beginning to expect their marriage to satisfy emotional needs as well. While this new conception of the "companionate marriage" ignored most of the gender inequalities which continued to characterize middle-class marriage relationships of the period, the notion that marriage should lead to emotional intimacy was nevertheless revolutionary in itself. As the novels discussed in this chapter make clear, middle-class women were coming to expect a matrimonial union in which they were fully the companions and confidantes of their husbands, a "republic of the spirit" in which both partners would respect each other's integrity and foster each other's emotional growth. And what would happen if marriage did not bring happiness? Increasingly, women of the Twenties and Thirties began to consider divorce.

CHAPTER THREE

Divorced Women

If one accepted the notion that marriage should lead to happiness and personal fulfillment, it logically followed that individuals were justified in dissolving unions which did not achieve these goals. And, increasingly, American women did just that. The divorce rate tripled in the United States between 1890 and 1920, continued to rise in the Twenties, and leveled off during the decade of the Depression before resuming its climb in the Forties and thereafter. (Woloch 1984, 542) If the majority of popular women writers embraced the concept of companionate marriage in their novels, they were more divided in their acceptance of its logical corolary: the right of a woman to dissolve her marriage if it did not fulfill her needs.

One popular novelist who was herself divorced was Edith Wharton, and divorce is as frequently the subject of her stories and novels as is marriage. Born in New York in 1862 into an era and a society which did not condone divorce, Wharton lived to see social attitude change, and this shift became the theme of one of her most acclaimed short stories, "Autres Temps . . . " (1911). Mrs. Lidcote divorced her husband years before the story opens and has been living in disgrace in Europe ever since. When she receives word that her daughter Leila has followed her example, she immediately sails home to lend the younger woman moral support. Much to her surprise, she finds that Leila's actions have been entirely condoned by society—while she herself remains under a cloud. As she explains to an old friend:

It's simply that society is much too busy to revise its own judgments. Probably no one . . . stopped to consider that my case and Leila's were identical. They only remembered that I'd done something which, at the time I did it, was condemned by society. My case has been passed on and classified: I'm the woman who has been cut for nearly twenty years. The older people have half forgotten why, and the younger ones have never really known: it's simply become a tradition to cut me. And traditions that have lost their meaning are the hardest of all to destroy. (279)

Although we are certainly meant to feel compassion for the divorced woman in this story, Wharton's purpose is to focus an ironic glance upon the inconsistencies of society rather than to pass judgment upon divorce itself.

Written two years before Edith Wharton divorced her husband, "Autres Temps . . ." is also an attempt on the part of the author to sort out her own feelings about divorce. As we have already noted, many of Wharton's stories in the first decade and a half of the century deal with women like Wharton herself, who are confined in marriages from which they long to escape. While Wharton evidently sympathized with the characters in these stories, some of whom grow desperate enough to leave their husbands, Wharton remained deeply ambivalent about divorce, even during the period in which she finally decided to divorce Teddy Wharton. As R.W.B. Lewis remarks, Edith Wharton "knew perfectly well that divorce had become common, even casual, among the younger American generation of the best society . . . [b]ut her own fifty-one-year-old character had been shaped by the conventions and pieties of a much older and narrower New York." (1975, 333) "Autres Temps . . ." speaks to this change in societal attitude; it does not necessarily condone divorce.

As Wharton's own divorce receded into her psychological past, the author's treatment of divorce in her fiction shifts somewhat. Wharton still evinces sympathy for Kate Clephane in *The Mother's Recompense* (1925), for example, who left her husband and small daughter nearly eighteen years before the novel begins. Nevertheless, as Cynthia Griffin Wolff observes, "although we are casually informed that Kate's marriage was endured in an atmosphere of stifling rigidity, we are not meant to infer that the limitations she confronted in any way justified her impetuous dash, though in some measure they explain it." (1977, 371) Kate's leaving of her husband has had devastating consequences for Kate. Even though she and her daughter Anne try to reestablish a close relationship, Kate has irrevocably lost the opportunity to be a mother to Anne. Kate eventually leaves Anne once again and returns to her lonely half-life among other expatriates on the Riviera.

In *Twilight Sleep* (1927) Wharton perhaps most explicitly offers her personal views on divorce. Pauline Manford is on her second marriage, having divorced her first husband "[i]n the early days of the new century [when] divorce had not become a social institution in New York." (25) By the time Pauline's daughter Nona has grown up, divorce has become commonplace. As Nona tells her mother, "Well—just look about you, mother! Don't they almost all get tired of each other? And when they do, will anything ever stop their having another try? Think of your big dinners! Doesn't Maisie always have to make out a list of previous marriages as long as a cross-word puzzle, to prevent your calling people by the wrong names?" (29) Much of the plot revolves around Nona's half brother Jim's futile attempts to retain the affections of his easily bored—and rather repellant— young wife Lita.[1] Pauline's middle-aged husband Dexter has, in turn, been growing tired of Pauline. When Dexter decides to "help" Jim by amusing Lita, the stage is set for disaster.

Wharton is at her most satirical in this novel and, of all the major characters, only Nona is presented sympathetically. As Dexter remarks of his daughter, "she had had her full share of the perpetual modern agitations. Yet Nona was firm as a rock: a man's heart could build on her." (126) One assumes that it is through Nona that Wharton presents her own opinions. While Nona seems to approve of divorce, railing against Aggie Heuston who refuses to release the husband she does not love so that he can marry Nona, she changes her mind when she sees the effect upon Jim of Lita's announcement that she wants a divorce. Distraught, Jim tells Nona he is ready to grant his wife her freedom, as he acknowledges Lita's right to be happy. Nona reflects, "That was the new idea of marriage, the view of Nona's contemporaries; it had been her own a few hours since. Now, seeing it in operation, she wondered if it still were. It was one thing to theorize on the detachability of human beings, another to watch them torn apart by the bleeding roots." (217)

By the 1920s, as Cynthia Griffin Wolff points out, Wharton's concerns had shifted from a concern over her inability to achieve the kind of marriage Dorothy Canfield espoused: a companionate marriage or a "republic of the spirit" inhabited by two individuals who love one another and whose interests and personalities are compatible. Instead, the late-middle-aged Wharton had begun to long for the family she had never had. In her later fiction, Wharton focuses more upon issues of parenting and upon the values of maintaining the stability of the family than upon the achievement of individual fulfillment. By the Twenties, Wharton explicitly defends the institution of marriage and points to the dangers of dissolving matrimonial ties through divorce. By the Twenties, Edith Wharton's message to her readers with regard to marriage and divorce has less in common with that articulated by Dorothy Canfield than, as we shall see, with the attitudes espoused by Margaret Ayer Barnes.

Born in Chicago in 1886 to parents who traced their ancestry back to English families who emigrated to the American colonies in the seventeenth century, Margaret Ayer Barnes majored in English and philosophy at Bryn Mawr and then returned to the Midwest to take her place in upper-middle-class Chicago, where she married, raised three sons, participated in amateur dramatics—and wrote a dramatization of Wharton's *The Age of Innocence*. Barnes produced only five novels, the first published in 1930, when the author was in her mid-forties, and the last appeared in 1938, when Barnes had reached her early fifties. *Years of Grace* (1930) proved to be Barnes' most critically acclaimed novel, winning the Pulitzer Prize for 1931. It was her most popular book as well, as it ranked fourth on the best-seller list in 1930 and fifth in 1931. Almost as popular was *Within This Present* (1933), which was among the top ten best-selling novels for 1934.[2]

Barnes' novels are fictional studies of marriage and divorce among people living in a social world not unlike the one which Barnes herself inhabited. Although the divorce rate fell slightly in the depths of the Depression in the early Thirties, it reversed itself and continued its upward climb later in the decade. (Ware 1982, 7) Middle-class women were increasingly likely to know people within their own social circles who had had a divorce, or even to have obtained a divorce themselves. Popular writers—and their public—could no longer dismiss divorce by pretending that it was something that only other women did. Nevertheless, greater familiarity with divorce did not breed less contempt for the institution. While many middle-class women in the Thirties were likely to be more empathetic than women in the Twenties toward those who had concluded that their marriages were intolerable, most continued to believe that divorce was wrong. In her novels, Barnes follows Wharton's lead in reflecting this more nuanced stance. Quite explicitly in some books, more obliquely in others, Barnes makes the case against divorce and for the indissolubility of marriage.

Edna His Wife (1935) is the only one of Barnes' novels which does not deal with characters contemplating—or obtaining—a divorce. It explores, instead, an unhappy marriage in which both spouses seem to have every reason for considering divorce. Edna Losser, daughter of a small-town railway stationmaster, marries the ambitious Paul Jones, a young lawyer who had thought to marry a woman would help him further his career. It is only too clear that Edna is not such a woman. She has inherited from her father "a complete absence of intellectual curiosity" (15), and she proves to be totally uninterested in current events, culture, or even Paul's legal cases. She is a liability to Paul in social situations, and Paul steadily betters his position solely through his own efforts. As Paul reaches the pinnacle of success, Edna finds herself the wife of a millionaire, living in an ultramodern—and sterile—New York penthouse, estranged from her husband, emotionally cut off from her two children, and separated from the friends she has been forced to leave behind as Paul has advanced up the social ladder.

Edna's marriage is a failure, for she and Paul are incompatible. Yet, Barnes never explicitly suggests that this couple should dissolve their marriage. In this novel, the author is more interested in portraying a woman caught in a trap from which she cannot escape than in resolving her protagonist's difficulties. As one reviewer remarked, "In 'Edna His Wife' Mrs. Barnes has done a difficult thing . . . she has recorded the painful history of a commonplace woman who is loyal, loving, and unselfish, and whose material reward for these virtues is abundant, but who is, in middle age, almost a symbol of futility." (*Saturday Review of Literature*, November 9, 1935, 7) The dull, unimaginative heroine gains stature through her dogged acceptance of a nearly untenable situation. We are meant to respect Edna's gallantry in coping with adversity; had she abandoned the struggle by divorcing her husband, she would have seemed a lesser woman.

If the protagonists refuse to solve their marital problems through divorce in *Edna His Wife*, the characters in *Westward Passage* (1931) appear at first to have no such inhibitions. Olivia Ottendorf divorced her first husband, an aspiring but impoverished novelist, to marry a millionaire admirer. Now, ten years after her second marriage, she reencounters her first husband, Nick Allen. A whirlwind courtship results. Nick persuades Olivia to leave her husband Harry and return to him. Olivia drives with Nick to his family farm where, in a matter of hours, she realizes that "she did not love Nick . . . It *had* been a dream. And now she was awake." (315) She leaves Nick and calls Harry to come and get her. The author suggests that the shallow, childish Olivia is finally growing up. The reader expects that she will now settle down and make Harry a good wife. Olivia may have made one big mistake in her life in marrying her first husband, but she has stopped herself from committing another by not divorcing her second husband.

In Barnes' three other novels, the writer is more candid in her disapproval of divorce. In *Years of Grace* (1930), she narrates events in Jane Ward's life, from childhood in the 1880s to late middle age in the 1920s. While Jane proves to have the strength and "grace" of character not to leave her husband for the man she loves, her daughter demonstrates a weaker resolve—and proceeds to do just what her mother had refrained from doing.

Tired of waiting for her childhood sweetheart to finish his beaux arts training and return from Europe to marry her, Jane chooses security over romance and weds Stephen Carter, and they settle down to a pleasant but uneventful life together. By the time she reaches her mid-thirties and has become the mother of three children, Jane realizes that she is slightly bored with her upper-middle-class suburban life. Like Marise Crittenden in Dorothy Canfield's *The Brimming Cup*, Jane is just in the frame of mind to be susceptible to the charms of another man. In this case, he is Jimmy Trent, impecunious husband of her best friend Agnes. Jimmy tries to persuade Jane to run away with him, but Jane feels an obligation to spare the feelings of her husband and her friend and she refuses. Thus, unlike Marise, who makes her decision based upon what is right for her, Jane forces herself to live up to her wedding vows, to do her "duty" to others regardless of her personal preferences. In this way, Jane's actions are closer to those of Edith Wharton's Newland Archer and Ellen Olenska, who sacrifice their personal happiness to preserve the stability of their social world. In *Years of Grace*,

Jimmy subsequently makes his way to Europe and enlists in the Prussian Army at the start of the Great War. Jane gets word that Jimmy has been killed at the front.

Some years later, as she thinks back over the sacrifices she has made in her life, Jane wonders what motivated her to make them. "Was it only to cultivate in your own character that intangible quality that Jane, for want of a better word, had defined as grace?" (577) Although Jane herself still concludes that such a goal has produced only a "barren reward" (577), Barnes suggests that Jane's life indeed has been a succession of "years of grace," that she has gallantly and courageously overcome temptation, maintained her self-respect and her integrity, and gained peace with herself. Like Archer's renunciation of Ellen, Jane's sacrifice has strengthened her character.

Social standards have changed, however, by the time that Jane's daughter Cicily has grown up, married, and had children of her own. Just as Edith Wharton probed the shifts in social attitudes toward divorce in a number of her works of fiction, so Barnes explores such changes here. Jane observes that Cicily's ideas about divorce are as different from Jane's own as Jane's were from her mother's: "In Jane's mother's time . . . a woman who was divorced, was an outcast, a public scandal, a skeleton in a family closet. In her time . . . she was a deplorable curiosity. . . . Now Cicily . . . regarded divorce as a practical aid to monogamous living." (468) When Cicily, like her mother before her, reaches the stage in which the "first fine careless rapture" of her marriage ends and boredom commences, she falls in love with another man, Albert Lancaster, who is married to Cicily's cousin Belle. Faced with essentially the same situation as was her mother before her, Cicily chooses differently: she is unwilling to sacrifice her happiness for the sake of her husband Jack and her cousin Belle. To her mother, who accuses Cicily of not caring "what havoc you make" (527), Cicily asserts that "[i]t's utter nonsense to think that if you love one man you can be happy living with another." (529) Jane, who has done just that, concludes that there "was something missing in the moral fiber of the rising generation. . . . It was a sex-ridden age." (534)

If Cicily emerges as a cool and "heartless" young woman who is too quick to sacrifice the happiness of her husband and her children to her own desires in *Years of Grace*,[3] in *Wisdom's Gate* (1938), the sequel to *Years of Grace*, we find that we may have misread Cicily's actions and motivations. Cicily here appears as a more sympathetic character, but, even though the story is now told from Cicily's point of view, we still are meant to view her decision to divorce Jack as a grave mistake. Now that we are privy to Cicily's inner thoughts, we discover that Cicily's divorce was more painful for her than she had admitted to her mother. Furthermore, we discover that Cicily finds that she is less certain she approves of divorce than she has led her mother to believe—or she has heretofore acknowledged even to herself.

In phrases reminiscent of Nona Manford's in *Twilight Sleep*, Cicily muses that "[d]ivorce, in the abstract, had always seemed to Cicily civilized, practical, necessary, and humane." (108) Yet, as divorce touches Cicily, her thinking changes, as does Nona's. Cicily's sophistication turns out to be only a facade. Underneath, she shares her mother's values; the standards of the two generations are not so far apart as it has seemed.

Not only do we learn in *Wisdom's Gate* that Cicily's divorce was more distressing than we had realized in *Years of Grace*, but we also discover that Cicily's marriage to Albert is not as successful as Cicily had anticipated it would be. Albert seemingly cannot help having affairs with other women, and Cicily begins to consider divorce a second time. However, *Wisdom's Gate* ends with the protagonist's having resolved that she will not make the same error twice: no matter how difficult her marriage may be, Cicily will not dissolve it. She has decided to stay with Albert, who assures her that he loves her and that he will always be true to her. Cicily is convinced of his love, but she knows that he won't be faithful to her. Finally aware that marriage is, at best, a compromise, Cicily concludes that "[n]othing was simple, except the fact that she loved him. To that simplicity she must confide her future." (370) Barnes suggests that Cicily has gained the maturity and insight her mother has had all along, that Cicily, too, has acquired the "grace" to confront and overcome her marital difficulties without resorting to divorce.

In *Within This Present* (1933), one of the minor characters from *Years of Grace* and *Wisdom's Gate* takes center stage—and proves that Jane and her daughter do not have a monopoly on matrimonial problems in their suburban upper-middle-class social circle. Young Sally Sewall marries Alan MacLeod on the eve of World War One. Although Sally and Alan are very much in love, their postwar life together is threatened, Barnes tells us, by the restlessness which has infected the war generation. When Alan returns to civilian life after the War, he cannot settle down; he feels trapped in his job as an executive at the Sewall family bank and bored with his suburban life-style. In such a state of mind, he is vulnerable to the calculating and self-centered Maisie, who finds Alan attractive and makes a determined play for him. Alan eventually realizes that he still loves Sally, and the two are sure that their life together will be better than before because now they must work together to confront a crisis—the onset of the Great Depression and the failure of the Sewall family bank. Sally tells Alan, "We'll have to work—for each other, Alan, and for the children—I know this sounds dreadfully moral—but there *is* something in morality." (606)

As Sally is cast as the "Betrayed Wife" rather than as the "Other Woman," divorce is presented unconditionally as a threat to the security of marriage. While *Within This Present* is perhaps Barnes' most candid statement on this subject, when Barnes' novels are read as a group it becomes clear that all five of her books present much the same message. In *Westward Passage* and

Wisdom's Gate, self-centered and thoughtless protagonists become unselfish, responsible adults only when they come to realize that divorce is not the answer to their problems. In *Edna His Wife*, the heroine valiantly endures an unhappy marriage, and in *Years of Grace* the central character stoically resists the temptation to leave her husband for another man in order to preserve the unity of her family. In an era in which readers were confronted by changing values and behaviors, Barnes provided them, in the words of one reviewer, with the "reassuring haven of the familiar and average." (Guy Holt, *Bookman*, September 1930, xvi)

As we have seen, Dorothy Canfield, Edith Wharton, and Margaret Ayer Barnes all portray characters who contemplate and sometimes break their matrimonial ties. While it is clear that Wharton and Barnes, at least, believe that it is better to make the best of even an imperfect marriage than to end it, none of these three writers are dogmatic in their defense of the institution of marriage. Even when they suggest that their protagonists who flirt with the notion of separation or divorce are in danger of making a wrong choice, these novelists treat their characters' dilemmas with compassion and sympathy.

Kathleen Norris, on the other hand, staunchly refuses to consider divorce as an option for her heroines, regardless of the circumstances. Given the volume of Norris' output, the length of her writing career, and the consistency with which she espoused her beliefs regarding the nature of marriage, it is possible to regard her as one of the most forceful and articulate proponents of a conservative conception of matrimony. A Norris heroine resolutely stands by her husband, no matter how difficult such an action may be. Perhaps in part because of Norris' Catholicism, divorce is never a choice for her characters. The Norris heroine considers no marital problem insupportable; she chooses to make the best of a bad situation rather than to contemplate escape through separation or divorce. As Barbara Atherton reflects in *Barberry Bush* (1929), "the die was cast. She was Barry du Spain's wife. Her life was beside him, to keep him happy if she could, to share his fame and prosperity if he were to win them, and, if not, to bring what courage and vision she might to her part in his failure." (127) Likewise, even though Rose Kirby, in *Rose of the World* (1924), discovers soon after her marriage that her husband is cold, calculating, and oppressive, Rose tells herself "that she has no choice but to make him as good a wife as was possible, and herself a successful and contented woman, if that might be." (230–231) Regardless of the difficulties confronting her married protagonists, Norris repeatedly counsels her readers that the marriage *can* be saved and that it is up to the wife to do so.

Kathleen Norris presents a decisively traditional attitude toward divorce, formulating much the same position as that held by popular women writers of previous generations. In Margaret Deland's *Philip and His Wife* (1894), it is "human selfishness" which prompts the protagonist to divorce his wife, and the story ends with all parties involved living unhappily ever after. (Riley 1991, 114) E.D.E.N. Southworth, the "Queen of the Domestic Novel" in the latter part of the nineteenth century (Nye 1970, 28), was a staunch supporter of the institution of marriage—and as firmly opposed to divorce. As women's historian Glenda Riley observes of Southworth in *Divorce: An American Tradition* (1991), "The troubles of distraught spouses filled the pages of her books during the 1880s and 1890s, but the solution was always separation. This parting was often followed by reconciliation, or the death of one spouse, which freed the other from the marital contract." (112) A voracious reader in her youth, Norris may well have read Southworth's novels. She certainly reflected similar attitudes toward marriage and divorce—and she employed the same plot device for extricating her heroines from the clutches of undesirable husbands. In *Rose of the World*, it eventually becomes clear that Rose's marriage to Clyde Bainbridge will never be a sound one: Rose comes to realize that her husband is going crazy, as his actions become increasingly irrational. After four years of exemplary behavior toward her deranged husband, Rose is suddenly released from her obligations, as Bainbridge plunges to his death in a quarry, freeing Rose to marry her childhood sweetheart. In *Barbarry Bush*, it turns out that the priest who married Barbara and Barry was an imposter. Their marriage is annulled, freeing Barbara to marry *her* childhood sweetheart. The reader is left with the impression that, if women will only accept their hardships, fate will eventually reward them for their patience. Thus, Norris' heroines, like Southworth's before them, often have it both ways: they reject divorce as a course of action and yet they find themselves liberated from their unhappy marriages.

The disparity in outlook among the writers we have considered in this chapter mirrors the continuity and change in public attitudes toward marriage and divorce in the early twentieth century. Kathleen Norris occupies a position at one end of the continuum: for Norris, marriage was a sacrament lasting "until death do us part." Given such thinking, divorce was obviously out of the question. As Rachael Gregory learns after her divorce from her first husband in Norris' *The Heart of Rachael* (1916), "No matter what the circumstances are, no matter where the right and wrong lie, divorce is wrong." (337) Dorothy Canfield, on the other hand, stands at the opposite end of the scale: if one has accepted the notion that marriage should lead to personal fulfillment, it logically follows that individuals are justified in dissolving a union which does not achieve this goal. In his 1939 survey of American divorce novels, James Harwood Barnett suggests that these "two antagonistic conceptions of marriage have existed side by side" (44) throughout the nineteenth and early twentieth centuries, one viewing marriage, as does Norris, as a "divine institution which was indissoluble in terms of human actions" and the other seeing marriage, as does Canfield, as a "human institution . . . [which] is to be valued as a means rather than as an end of human life" and which could be terminated at will. (47) While Barnett asserts that the latter notion had gradually gained ascendency over the former by the early twentieth century, he suggests that the more traditional attitude had by no means died out. Thus, popular women novelists as dissimilar in their outlook as Canfield and Norris reflect attitudes toward marriage and divorce held by different factions of the reading public in the early twentieth century.

It would be a mistake to suggest that the middle-class readers of popular novels held logically consistent, clear-cut positions on marriage and divorce. Quite possibly, many readers espoused views in which both traditional and modern notions jostled one another in uneasy proximity. In her study of marriage and divorce in the late nineteenth and early twentieth centuries, social historian Elaine Tyler May suggests that many couples in the Twenties and Thirties were "caught between traditions of the past and visions of the future." (1980, 158) Like their parents and grandparents before them, they still believed that men and women should occupy separate marital spheres: that husbands should work to provide for their families and that wives should keep house and raise the children. At the same time, they also held the somewhat contradictory notion that marriage should not primarily be based upon duties and sacrifices but should be an opportunity for personal satisfaction; they believed that marriage should promote happiness, that matrimony should lead to fun and excitement. May contends that the increased divorce rate during this period resulted in part from this tendency to invest marriage with mutually incompatible expectations. Thus, May places Barnett's "antagonistic conceptions of marriage" within the individuals themselves. The popular novelist who perhaps best conforms to May's description is Temple Bailey. A firm believer in the cult of domesticity and the sanctity of marriage, Bailey nevertheless subscribed to the notion that marriage should lead to the mutual happiness of husband and wife. It logically follows that individuals would be justified in dissolving a union which did not achieve this goal. Bailey sidesteps this issue by permitting her heroines to realize their mistakes before the wedding bells have pealed: there are a number of broken engagements in her books, but no broken marriages. As each of Bailey's heroines eventually marries the "right" man and, consequently, every heroine's marriage is a success, there is no reason for divorce in Bailey's novels.

Margaret Ayer Barnes and Edith Wharton stake out a middle position on marriage which is perhaps closer to Norris' than to Canfield's. While Barnes and Wharton are more tolerant of those characters who have left or divorced their spouses than Norris could be, they are nevertheless adamant in suggesting that it is more important for a protagonist to preserve his or her marriage than for the character to attempt to gain personal happiness. In fact, they suggest, persevering in their marital duties and responsibilities provides people with the "opportunity to grow through enduring what must be endured." (Stein 1984, 218) Thus, Wharton's Newland Archer and Barnes' Jane Ward Carter are better people for having placed the welfare of their families before their own interests. If Kathleen Norris views marriage as a religious sacrament, Wharton and Barnes view it as a social contract. Norris' characters cannot contemplate divorce because such an action would be morally wrong; Wharton's and Barnes' protagonists cannot sunder their marriages without repudiating the society of which they are a part. It is clear that, although the popular novelists of the day leaned toward a relatively traditional view of marriage and divorce, there was considerable difference of opinion regarding the nature of marriage and the morality of divorce.

CHAPTER FOUR

Women at Work

The majority of best-selling women novelists of the Twenties and Thirties, like Kathleen Norris and Temple Bailey, appear to have assumed that women's work was home work. Most female writers constructed a fictional universe in which only men were bread-winners, while women remained at home, caring for the children and keeping house. The "good" wife was the wife who shouldered her domestic duties willingly and competently. Popular women writers thus reflected the attitudes of the public at large, who continued to uphold an "economic concept" of marriage, "requiring the husband's support and the wife's service to him"—as mother and housewife. (Cott 1987, 210)

Norris and Bailey were not the only ones to support the cult of domesticity. In pioneer novelist Bess Streeter Aldrich's *Spring Came on Forever* (1935), the villainess's refusal to carry out her domestic responsibilities points to her utter unsuitability as a wife—and to serious character flaws as well. Although Joe Holmsdorfer is all but pledged to Rose Schaffer, who is "pretty, neat and clean, [and] so pleasant to every one" (188), when schoolteacher Myrtie Bates comes to board with the Schaffers, she sets her cap for Joe and quickly wins his affections. It is not long before Joe wishes that he had married Rose instead of Myrtie. His new wife asserts that her domestic duties are too tiring for her, thus forcing Joe to hire servants to do her housework, and she continually demands that Joe live beyond his means in order to provide her with luxuries. In her farm novels Gladys Hasty Carroll presents protagonists who possess all the housewifely virtues that Aldrich's Myrtie Bates lacks. In *As the Earth Turns* (1933), young Jen Shaw is a born homemaker, who works from dawn to night and yet has the "knack, people said, of looking rested." (64) As we shall see in the following chapter, Jen not only discharges her domestic chores capably but also is thoroughly accepting of males and females performing gender-specific tasks. Although her future husband seems to "know no difference between men's and women's places" (301), Jen herself regards his views as a sign of eccentricity.

Not all popular women novelists held such conventional beliefs regarding a married woman's proper role. As discussed in a previous chapter, Dorothy Canfield explicitly challenges received wisdom in both *The Squirrel-Cage* (1912) and *The Home-Maker* (1924). Not only does Canfield suggest that husband and wife should share—or even exchange—the duties and responsibilities that society had traditionally assigned them, but she also advances the unorthodox idea that the less time and effort a woman spends on housework the better a wife and mother she is likely to be. In *The Home-Maker*, Evangeline Knapp is endlessly scrubbing the floors, polishing the furniture, beating the rugs, and, even though she, like her friend Mattie Farnham, automatically believes that "[h]ome-making is the noblest work anybody can do!" (199) the truth of the matter is that Eve Knapp hates housework. Because she forces herself to lavish so much of her energy on homemaking, she has no reserves of patience left to expend upon her husband and children. Lydia Emery in Canfield's *The Squirrel-Cage* is not a born housewife, as are the heroines in Norris', Aldrich's, and Carroll's novels; neither is she a model—if reluctant—homemaker, as is Eve Knapp. When Lydia is left in charge of her parents' household upon her mother's illness, she proves to be an indifferent mistress. Her father is "dismayed by the thorough-going domestic anarchy that had ensued. He was partly aware that what alarmed him most was Lydia's lack of zest in the battle . . . [signaling a] failure to acquiesce in the normal, usual standard of values." (80) While a Norris heroine would be likely to come to realize the importance of domestic order and mend her ways, Canfield presents Lydia's lack of interest in housekeeping as a sensible response to an unreasonable social expectation. As Lydia believes that housework demands too great a share of a woman's time, she tries to convince her *fiancé* to build their house so that it can be maintained easily—to omit carved hall panels, for example, which will be difficult to dust. Paul ignores Lydia's entreaties, as his primary goal is to construct an ornate structure assertive of his social status. Once married, Lydia confronts "all of the dismaying difficulties of housekeeping and keeping up a social position in America." (194) Lydia feels increasingly smothered by her homemaking responsibilities, and it is only Paul's death which relieves her of her burden.

While Canfield questions the emphasis that should be placed upon housework, and even hints that in some cases it may be appropriate for women to transfer their duties in the home to others and to enter the paid labor force, few other popular women novelists appear to have agreed with her. Most other writers, as we have seen, maintain that a woman's place is in the home, carrying out her traditional wifely responsibilities. In actuality, according to the U.S. Census of 1930, almost ninety percent of all married women did remain at home rather than enter the workplace. (Cott 1987, 182) For that matter, most unmarried women stayed home as well. In the Twenties and Thirties, only about a quarter of the female population were wage earners. As the novels of the era indicate, most young, single, middle-class women were not expected to support themselves; like Lydia Emery, they were to move gracefully from their fathers' to their husbands' homes without ever being forced to venture out into the world of work. Even those middle-class families hard put to make ends meet were reluctant to send their unmarried daughters out into the work force or to encourage them to prepare themselves for gainful employment. In Kathleen Norris' *The American Flaggs* (1936), twenty-two-year-old Penelope Fitzpercy is dissatisfied with the shabbiness of her home and embarrassed by her mother's inability to pay bills on time. Penelope reflects, "I'd like—any change, more shame to me! I've tried to get work; I'm not trained for anything. I've never made any money except a dollar or two earned selling books or candlesticks." (87) Eventually Penelope elects to improve her lot through the traditional avenue open to women: she marries money.

But what future awaits the woman who cannot attract a prosperous husband—or even a penniless one? Zona Gale explores the life of such a woman in *Miss Lulu Bett* (1920). Born in Portage, Wisconsin, in the 1870s, Gale's stories, novels, and plays were frequently set in small Midwestern towns. Although her earlier work tended toward sentimentality, her tone had changed by the early 'teens as Gale herself became active with the Women's Peace Party, woman suffrage, and La Follette Progressivism. Winner of the Pulitzer Prize in 1920, *Miss Lulu Bett* was soon transformed into a play, which in turn boosted book sales. Published the same year as Sinclair Lewis' *Main Street*, this novel, too, is an attack upon the complacency and provincialism of small-town America. At the beginning of the story, thirty-four-year-old Lulu Bett is living with her younger sister Ina and her sister's husband Dwight Deacon. Gale deftly describes Lulu's position in the family:

There emerged from the fringe of things, where she perpetually hovered, Mrs. Deacon's older sister, Lulu Bett, who was "making her home with us." And that was precisely the case. *They* were not making her a home, goodness knows. Lulu was the family beast of burden. (3–4)

Lulu cooks, cleans, and washes the dishes. When the Deacons' spoiled daughter Monona refuses to eat her dinner, it is Lulu's meal that grows cold while Lulu hurries to the kitchen to prepare milk toast for her niece. When the family goes on a picnic, it is Lulu who prepares the basket and then serves the meal at the river's edge. Gale paints Lulu's life as one of never-ending drudgery. Her situation is made worse by the fact that

Dwight Deacon, a petty, self-important tyrant, continually teases Lulu to the point of cruelty, supported by Ina, who makes it a practice never to disagree with her husband. Perhaps because Lulu has been incapable of "capturing" a husband, she has no self-confidence or self-assertiveness; thus, she never tries to stand up for herself against Dwight's verbal on-slaughts.

Through a rather improbable turn of events, Lulu gradually comes to see her situation more clearly—and more critically. She begins to assert herself. She defends herself when Dwight tries to ridicule her. She extricates herself from her position as the Deacons' unpaid—and unappreciated—housekeeper by taking a job in a bakery. She takes an interest in Neil Cornish, a new man in town who opens a music shop above Dwight's dentist office. When Cornish confesses that he is lonely and asks Lulu to marry him, she accepts. By the end of the novel, she has embarked upon a new, more satisfying existence as a married woman whose husband, Gale leads the reader to believe, will fully appreciate Lulu's accomplishments and cherish her as his wife. Having thus freed herself from her oppressive and dreary life as spinster "dependant," Lulu Bett has narrowly escaped the common fate of the middle-class single woman who has no skills to offer in the marketplace.

Eighteen-year-old Bea Chipley, in Fannie Hurst's *Imitation of Life* (1933), is equally unprepared to make her own living. Soon after her mother dies, Bea begins to worry about the health of her father, a salesman for a large pickle-and-relish company. Bea has no relatives to take her in if her father should die. She wonders, "What happened to girls thrown on their own resources? They worked, of course. If only Mother had not opposed the kindergarten course." (15) Mrs. Chipley had taught her daughter that "nice girls" worked only for "pin money and not through necessity." (16) But what if circumstances dictate that Bea must work for "necessity"? Fearful of the future, Bea marries Mr. Pullman, the family boarder, in order to regain a sense of the "indefinable security which comes with a home of one's own." (28)

For Bea, as for other fictional—and real-life—women of the day, mar-riage is not a guarantee of economic safety. When Mr. Pullman unexpect-edly dies in a railway accident, Bea must support herself and her young daughter. In such a situation, society condoned a woman's efforts to earn her own living—as long as she confined herself to fields traditionally regarded as "women's" work, such as school teaching or stenography. When Bea tries to persuade the pickle company to allow her to assume her father's sales job, the company refuses, telling her that they do not hire women. With the help of her black housekeeper Delilah, Bea opens a chain of waffle shops and eventually becomes one of the richest and most successful businesswomen in the country. Although Hurst seems at first to be presenting a career woman whose extraordinary talent for commerce sets her apart from other fictional heroines of the era, in fact, Bea is quite conventional at heart. Like most other working women of the period, Bea does not regard her work as a "career" but as a job she has undertaken solely to support her family. It was not her choice to enter the labor market, and what Bea the brilliant businesswoman wants most in life is to remarry and settle down with the man she loves.

Ella Bishop in Bess Streeter Aldrich's *Miss Bishop* (1933) also yearns for marriage. She dreams of a "little house in a garden and red firelight and . . . the man I love . . . and children." (26) But, through a combination of bad luck and malevolent human intervention, Ella must settle for a life as an English teacher in the "pioneer" phase of the newly opened state university. Ella is more than an educator; she is also a surrogate mother for generations of university students. Aldrich tells us that she "assisted them all,—boys and girls alike. She helped them about participles and finances, adverbial phrases and clothes, split infinitives and bodily aliments, clauses and morals." (128) Upon Ella's retirement her former students return to campus to pay tribute to her. Now influential leaders of the state—a U.S. senator, a prominent minister, a wealthy businessman, a mechanical engineer, the chairman of the university's board of directors—every one asserts that Miss Bishop influenced his life, that his present success is due in part to her compassionate guidance. Although Miss Bishop may have been disappointed in her desire for a husband and children of her own, she finally realizes that the life she has led has been equally rewarding. She has faithfully discharged the mission given her by the college president early in her tenure, a mission which he describes as being "something like carrying a torch to light the paths for all the boys and girls with whom you come into contact." (102)

Miss Bishop may have enjoyed a successful "career," but her example is hardly one which challenges conventional notions regarding a woman's proper place. Ella Bishop's initial plan is to enter the work force only until her marriage, an event which she hopes will be soon in coming. She trains as a teacher because "[t]o clerk in a store, do housework, or teach school were the only three [acceptable] avenues open to any girl." (38) As a teacher, she carries out activities generally associated with mothering: she instructs her charges and she provides them with emotional and moral guidance. Ella Bishop may never have married and raised a family of her own, but, over a half-century of teaching, she has become a "mother of students." (332) In this novel, the boundary between the home and the workplace is all but erased.

As the above examples demonstrate, single middle-class women may have regarded work outside the home as a distinctly second-best alternative to marriage as a lifelong occupation, but society certainly condoned paid employment as a temporary activity for young women prior to marriage. The nineteenth-century prejudice against single women working had substantially weakened by the Twenties and Thirties, as growing numbers of young middle-class women for the first time joined working-class women in the work force. And in novel after novel published during this period, both working- class and middle-class protagonists hold paying jobs before they marry. Working-class characters are domestics, typists, and department store clerks, reflecting the fact that by 1930, as William Chafe has observed, "almost 2 million women were employed as secretaries, typists, and file clerks, and another 700,000 worked as salesgirls in department stores." (1972, 50) In one of the few best-selling novels of the period to focus upon a working-class protagonist, the heroine is a domestic, still one of the primary forms of paid employment for women at the bottom of the socioeconomic ladder. In *Lummox* (1923) Fannie Hurst lashes out against the ill-treatment of domestic workers. Born in 1889 to middle-class Jewish parents of German descent, Hurst grew up in St. Louis, Missouri. In order to gain experience for writing, she moved to New York City in 1910, "taking bit parts in plays, working in department stores, restaurants, and factories and poking around in tenement districts, trying to observe life 'the way Dickens did,' " (Kinsman 1975, 313) Out of Hurst's encounters with the metropolis came *Lummox*. A social novel which focuses upon the inequalities and injustices resulting from a class-based society, *Lummox* vividly depicts the living and working conditions of the main character and her coworkers. Forced to labor long hours for little pay, the women are housed in damp cellars or ill-ventilated attics and fed scraps from the families' tables. They are hired as though they were animals: prospective employers check their teeth, feel their muscles, examine their scalps. Having signed no contract, they have no legal recourse should their master or mistress decide in a moment of anger or pique to dispense with their services.

Middle-class characters hold more responsible positions—and are treated with more respect by their employers and the community. Many are schoolteachers, and the high proportion of middle-class protagonists depicted as teachers parallels real-life trends: by 1920, the teaching profession had become eighty-five percent female. Other middle-class heroines are secretaries and stenographers, governesses and housekeepers.

In all of these occupations, as in teaching, women frequently replicated their role in the home. As office workers, for example, Nancy F. Cott observes, "women could advance in their careers only by retreating, in effect, to the professional performance of the wifely adjunct role." (1987, 190) Faith Baldwin presents such a situation in *The Office Wife* (1930). Hardworking advertising executive Lawrence Fellows is married, but he spends more time at the office in the company of his personal secretary than he does at home with his wife. Anne Murdock becomes Fellows' secretary after her predecessor, a middle-aged spinster who had fallen in love with him, has a nervous breakdown. Murdock attends to Fellows' professional needs, worries about his health, and organizes his social affairs. She has become an "office wife." Anne discovers that she, too, is in love with her boss. Eventually, Fellows' wife divorces him for another man, leaving Fellows free to wed Anne. She wants to continue as his secretary once they are married, but Fellows vetoes the idea. Anne reflects—somewhat dubiously—that she will be "[n]o longer—the Office Wife. Just—Wife. That was better, of course, more wonderful, complete, perfect. Yet—" (277)

Society expected that working women would retire from the labor force upon marriage, and most of the heroines of popular women's novels of the period—Anne Murdock included— do just that. Anne is one of the few to be ambivalent about leaving her job; generally, working heroines serve notice without experiencing even a single pang of regret: married women need to devote all of their time and attention to their homes and their families, and that is that. And yet . . . some protagonists are not completely happy as homemakers. In Vina Delmar's *Bad Girl*, (1928) Dot Haley finds that she has more time on her hands than she knows what to do with, once she becomes Mrs. Eddie Collins, Unemployed Housewife. She begins to wonder, "What did one do with unoccupied days that stretched along with tedious consistency?" (1928, 81) When she hints to Eddie that she might return to work, her husband's response is a decisive refusal: "No, God damn it. What the hell do you think I am that I can't support my wife? Go to the movies, visit your friends, do what you please, but you'll not go to work." (83) Dot's boredom is soon dispelled when she and Eddie move from a furnished room to an unfurnished apartment, a change in situation which affords Dot the opportunity to busy herself arranging and cleaning her new home. Soon after the move, Dot becomes pregnant. She thinks no more of going back to work.[1]

When Ed Shaw marries country schoolteacher Margaret Ross in Gladys Hasty Carroll's *As the Earth Turns* (1933), Margaret stays on to finish the last few months of the term, as the school committee is unable to find a replacement. Like Eddie Collins, Ed Shaw is dead set against a wife of his working, even temporarily, believing that her doing so suggests he is not a good husband, that he is unable to carry out his most basic duty: that of providing for his family. Collins' and Shaw's strong conviction that their wives should not work reflects the belief among white middle-class Americans of the time that a "working wife placed a stigma upon the husband and the family." (Wandersee 1981, 83) As Ed Shaw complains to his wife, "Anyone would think I couldn't keep a wife, and when I got one she had to work out to help support herself. It's something I never thought I'd come to, having to let the neighbors believe I couldn't feed my family—" (Carroll 1933, 120–21) It is only when Margaret gives in to her husband and offers to serve notice before the end of the school year that Ed magnanimously allows her to finish the term. Margaret has appealed to something even more basic to Ed's conception of his role as husband than his image of the male as breadwinner: his perception of himself as head of the household, maker of final decisions. Thus flattered, he gives in to Margaret, who has learned from this incident that "[i]t must always come to this in the end; she must do as Ed wanted and do it happily, not complainingly; she must see things as he saw them; for Ed there was only one way." (124)

In several novels written by Faith Baldwin, whose *Office Wife* is mentioned above, the wife keeps her job after marriage. Baldwin, a founder and faculty member of the Famous Writers School in Westport, Connecticut, was an extremely popular writer in her day, ranking "next to Kathleen Norris in her field, both in prolificness and in financial returns." (Harte and Riley 1969, 65) In Baldwin's *Week-End Marriage* (1932), released as a film by First National the same year, Lola Davis insists on continuing to work after her marriage to Kenneth Hayes. Lola asserts that theirs will be a "fifty-fifty marriage," a "partnership." (21) Although Ken, who is earning fifty dollars a week as a salesman in a public utility company to Lola's thirty-five-dollars a week as a secretary, is troubled by Lola's decision, things go relatively smoothly in the first months of their life together. But Lola is always tired after work and they frequently have deli dinners rather than home cooking. (Lola, it goes without saying, is responsible for the cooking and housework even though they are both working.) When Lola begins to earn more than Ken does, however, their marriage starts to disintegrate. No longer the primary provider, Kenneth is unable to maintain his self-respect. He spends more and more time playing poker and getting drunk. He loses his job.

When Lola announces that she has a chance for a promotion in St. Louis, she asks Ken to move there with her. Kenneth refuses, and he might be speaking for most middle-class husbands of the period when he asserts:

When I married you I expected a wife. But you thought more of your goddam job and your pin-money and your—earning capacity. . . . The sort of wife I knew anything about, and was a fool to expect, worked with and for her man all right. But not in an office. She did her job at home. And she did it well. And she made a man feel that he had something to come home to besides a worn-out, grouchy girl, thinking of nothing but money and career. (200)

Lola refuses to conform to Ken's expectations, and they separate. Kenneth opens a gas station with a friend; slowly it begins to make money. Lola finally comes to realize that she is going to have to choose between Ken and her career. Like most middle-class women of the era, she decides her marriage is more important to her than her job, so she returns to New York to become a full-time wife.

In Katharine Brush's *Young Man of Manhattan* (1930), Toby McLean is likewise unable to accept a wife who is more successful in her job than is McLean himself. Brush, who began her career as a motion picture columnist and married a newspaperman in 1920, may have been drawing upon her own experience in this novel when she has Toby, a sportswriter for the *New*

York Star, meet Ann Vaughn, a movie columnist for the *Chronicle-Press*. It is love at first sight and Toby promptly proposes. He promises her,

I wouldn't try to run your life for you. I believe in individuals, Ann. You're one—if there ever was one—and I'd respect that. Always. I'd respect your work, and your time, and your right to do as you chose. If you felt like keeping your job, you could. If you didn't, you wouldn't need to. . . . You'd be free, do you see? Free as you are now. (300)

Toby and Ann do marry, Ann does continue to work, and marital friction develops almost immediately. Toby is jealous of Ann's career, which progresses more rapidly than does his. They have their first quarrel, and they make up only when Ann assures Toby that, although she may be doing better than he, Toby is the more talented writer. Although Toby insists that they will live on his income, it is soon apparent that they cannot. Ann offers to help out with the finances, but Toby refuses: "What would she think of him then as a protector and provider? And what would he think of himself?" (73)

The reader begins to realize that Toby McLean's perception of his marital role is not so different from that of an Ed Shaw or Eddie Collins. Though he is willing to "allow" his wife to continue to work, she is to do so only to satisfy her need for personal fulfillment and to earn "pin money." She is not to work because of economic need; Toby alone is to provide the financial support for the household.

Domestic tensions mount, and the couple drifts perilously close to a divorce. The situation is saved only when Toby forces himself to settle down to do some serious writing. Toby quits his job on the newspaper to become a writer of fiction and soon earns large sums of money. Now that there is no longer any doubt that Toby is the spouse with the more prestigious and lucrative career, it appears that the couple's troubles are over. Ann is able to keep her job, as she no longer poses a psychological threat to her husband.

For Brush herself, the situation was not resolved so tidily: she divorced her first husband in 1928, remarried in 1929, and published *Young Man of Manhattan* in 1930. During her second marriage, she became a best-selling and prosperous novelist and short-story writer, as well as a Hollywood scriptwriter. Despite the fact that her second husband was a banker and economist and presumably did not feel as directly threatened by his wife's literary success as did her first husband, Brush's second marriage also ended in divorce in 1941.

In both *Week-End Marriage* and *Young Man of Manhattan*, the issue is not so much the fact that the wife works but that she is more successful than her husband. In each novel the issue nearly breaks up the marriage. Ken and Lola's relationship is saved only by Lola's quitting her job; Ann manages to keep her position as well as her marriage only because Toby's earnings eventually exceed her own. No simple solution presents itself to rescue Barbara Jackson and Henricks Smith's marriage in Janet Ayer Fairbank's *Rich Man, Poor Man* (1936). Sister of novelist Margaret Ayer Barnes, Fairbank was educated in private schools and attended the University of Chicago. She married Kellogg Fairbank in 1900 and bore three children; in 1910 she published her first book. In just over six hundred pages of *Rich Man, Poor Man*, Fairbank's sixth—and last—novel, the author follows the lives of her protagonists from the Republican Presidential Convention of 1908 to the eve of the Great Depression. While Barbara Jackson's political activism is modeled upon the author—Fairbank campaigned for woman suffrage, held office in the Progressive Party, and later was a Democratic national committeewoman—Henricks Smith is drawn as coming from the same upper-class Chicago social circle as Fairbank did. Though the tension in the novel emerges from the characters' dissimilar interests and backgrounds, the fact that Fairbank shared primary traits with each of her protagonists compelled her to treat both Barbara and Henricks with compassion.

When Henricks first meets Barbara in the summer of 1908, she is a small-town librarian in Kansas and an impassioned, effective orator for the Progressive campaign. Barbara's political philosophy has been shaped by Midwestern populism as well as by a growing commitment to feminism, and she is used to thinking for herself and being treated as an equal by both women and men. Henricks respects Barbara's desire to effect social and political change almost as much as he admires her beauty. After their marriage he makes no attempt to prevent her involvement in the suffrage movement, even though he comes to find his wife's passionate pursuit of the issue rather narrow-minded. His relatives, meanwhile, disapprove of Barbara's disinclination to take seriously her duties as homemaker and hostess.

In this novel, it is difficult to disentangle the marital problems stemming from Barbara's determination to continue her political career from the tensions arising from the spouses' disparity in social background. Barbara comes from a family of modest means, while Henricks is the son of a prominent Chicago bank president. Barbara never feels comfortable in her role as society matron and, soon after the War, the Smiths divorce. Barbara marries a working- class radical whom she meets in Greenwich Village, and Henricks marries a woman from his own class, a distant relative and family friend with whom he had grown up, who makes him a perfect wife. Unlike Barbara, she "managed his house as well as she did him: in town and in the country both he had charming, well-run establishments." (624)

Fairbank may have herself supported women's involvement in politics, but Barbara's characterization suggests that the author is ambivalent regarding the issue of married women working, especially if these women are feminists who place career before marriage. At the beginning of the novel, Fairbank presents Barbara as a capable, idealistic woman of integrity who loves her husband and tries to conform to his family's expectations of her while yet attempting to preserve some of her own principles and values. Her husband seems sympathetic to her efforts, and their marriage appears to be fairly successful, despite differences in social class and in the intensity of their political commitment. Gradually, however, Barbara is presented as becoming more and more obsessed with her public interests. Once the couple has separated and Barbara has moved to Greenwich Village, Fairbank observes that she "had changed to an astonishing extent. She was much more combative than she had been before, and she considered herself an authority on various matters about which her husband suspected she knew very little." (595–96) It is not so much Barbara's superficial grasp of political issues or her increasing intolerance that are the worst results of her almost fanatical determination to continue her career; it is the deleterious effect of her political activity upon her husband and her child. Barbara refuses to help to further or even to condone her husband's career: banking, in Barbara's eyes, is not a socially useful profession. Even worse, Fairbank suggests, is Barbara's neglect of her daughter. It is Henricks, not Barbara, who is the child's primary parent, and Henricks gains custody of their daughter after the divorce.

By this point in the novel, the author seems to be mounting an antifeminist attack, arguing that such a woman's career indeed threatens her marriage, that a woman's place is in the home, providing moral and emotional support to her husband, and care and nurture to her children. Barbara seems to have failed in her most basic responsibilities. Furthermore, she appears to have done so not in the courageous pursuit of a justified goal but out of a wrongheaded, misguided allegiance to a trivial crusade.

And yet, Fairbank cannot leave it at that. At the very end of the novel, she almost grudgingly rehabilitates Barbara's reputation. Several years after the divorce, Henricks happens upon Barbara, who is giving a speech in Manhattan's Union Square. He listens, unobserved, and reflects of Barbara that "[s]habby and courageous and dedicated, she emphasized a side of life which was less self- interested than his own, and possibly quite as well worth while." (626) Barbara's professional commitment may well have contributed to the breakup of her marriage, the outcome contemporary critics darkly predicted would result from married women pursuing independent careers, but at least the author stops short of saying that Barbara's neglect of her husband and daughter has resulted from completely selfish motives.

As we have seen, most of the popular novels of the period have depicted women who do not work at all or, if they do, who resign from their jobs upon marriage. In very few novels have the heroines attempted to remain in the labor force as working wives, and such cases have inevitably led to marital tensions. In only one best seller of the period, Dorothy Canfield's

The Home-Maker (1924), which we have discussed earlier, does the wife not only become a wage earner but the sole breadwinner of the family while her husband assumes care of the home and the children. Fully aware of public attitudes regarding the proper roles of husband and wife in the Twenties, even Canfield does not construct a plot in which the spouses take the initiative in deciding to exchange responsibilities; instead, it is fate which intervenes in prompting them to take on each other's roles. And it is fortunate that fate does intervene for, in *The Home-Maker*, Canfield introduces us to a wife who is a much better businessperson than her husband. Eva Knapp's ability is rewarded, and she is soon earning more money than Lester ever did—a fictional turn of events seldom duplicated in real life, where few wives could hope to equal or even approximate the wages their husbands could earn.

Despite Canfield's belief that couples should decide for themselves how best to allocate their responsibilities, few men and women in the Twenties and Thirties were prepared to abandon the notion that the woman's place was in the home. When men lost their jobs during the Depression and women were forced to become the family's only breadwinner, this by no means meant that the husbands therefore took over their wives' traditional duties. Instead, working women shouldered two jobs, continuing to carry out their domestic work even as they temporarily took on their husbands' role as financial provider. As Winifred D. Wandersee has observed in *Women's Work and Family Values, 1920–1940* (1981), "[f]amily studies done during the Depression present no cases in which the husband took over the household and child care responsibilities, although some men offered greater or lesser degrees of help to their working wives." (107) The fact that American commitment to the notion of separate spheres of marital influence and obligation remained so strong, even during the Depression, a crisis situation in which one might expect traditional beliefs and assumptions to be modified or even overturned, indicates that long-accepted outlooks on marriage likewise retained their hold. And in the popular women's novels of the day, despite some questioning of established mores by the likes of Dorothy Canfield, most writers continued to depict couples who replicated the customary allocation of duties and responsibilities: in popular fiction as in real life, the woman's place remained in the home.

CHAPTER FIVE

Farming and Pioneer Women

As we have seen, female protagonists entered the labor force in ever-increasing number in women's popular novels of the Twenties and Thirties, reflecting the fact that job opportunities for middle-class women were growing. Even if more women than ever before were becoming paid workers, however, most still remained at home. And for a substantial proportion of women, home was a farm. Even though the number of farmers was steadily falling by the Twenties, more Americans tilled the soil during this period than engaged in any other occupation. Women helped their husbands work the land or, if necessary, managed farms by themselves.

During the 1920s and 1930s, the American book market was flooded with scores of farm novels, many of which were written by women. Some women novelists placed their protagonists in contemporary settings. Gladys Hasty Carroll, for example, detailed the daily routines of farm life in rural Maine in *As the Earth Turns* (1933) and *A Few Foolish Ones* (1935), while Josephine Johnson presented a grim account of the impact of the Great Depression upon a Missouri farm family in *Now in November* (1934). Other writers focused their attention upon the frontier regions of the past and upon the pioneer women and men who first settled these virgin lands. Following the lead of Willa Cather, whose *O Pioneers!* (1913) and *My Antonia* (1918) chronicled the lives of immigrant settlers upon the Nebraska prairies in the late nineteenth century, Edna Ferber, Bess Streeter Aldrich, Elizabeth Madox Roberts, Rose Wilder Lane, and Caroline Miller likewise focused upon pioneer heroines and heroes who endure great hardship in their struggle to transform the wilderness into farmland.

Farm and frontier novels are, by and large, a phenomenon of the Twenties and Thirties; it is during these decades that the genre flourished. Why would such novels appear in quantity then—and not earlier or later? In *The Middle Western Farm Novel in the Twentieth Century* (1965), Roy W. Meyer addresses this question. For one thing, Meyer notes, the closing of the frontier, marked by Frederick Jackson Turner's announcement of the fact in 1893, stimulated nostalgic interest in frontier issues and led to the creation of two popular literary genres. One, the Western, emerged with the publication of Owen Wister's *The Virginian* in 1902. The other, the farm novel, dates its inception back to Hamlin Garland's *Main-Traveled Roads* of 1891. While writers of Westerns celebrated the cowboy's freedom from the confining pressures exerted by farmers, women, and towns and set their stories in the era just before the frontier was settled; farm novelists celebrated the victory of the pioneer farmer over the land—the civilizing of the frontier—and set their novels in the period during which the frontier irrevocably lost its frontier character to become farmland.

Also, Meyer surmises, both writers and readers of farm novels tended to have begun their lives on the farm and to have later moved from rural area to town or city. In the first three decades of the twentieth century, farmers and their children moved off the land and into towns and cities in record number. By the time of the U.S. census of 1920, over half of the American population was listed for the first time as urban rather than rural. The move from farm to town afforded many writers the opportunity to attain perspective upon their early experiences, and these events formed the basis for their stories and novels. At the same time, transplanted farming families, now freed from the daily round of farm chores from dawn to dusk, had more time to read. According to Meyer, it was in part the demographic shift of farmers from the country to the town or city which stimulated reader interest in novels detailing rural life. Yet, Meyer cautions, the audience for such books was short-lived; once those who had firsthand knowledge of farm life died, much of the interest in such subjects faded as well. Likewise, the number of writers who remembered the settling of the prairies or who had grown up on the farm began to diminish. Thus, by the 1940s, the outpouring of farm-based novels slowed to a trickle.

Perhaps one of the greatest attractions of novels set on the farm or on the frontier for readers of the Twenties and Thirties is the fact that such novels were fictional representations of one of our most strongly held cultural myths, the belief that "in America, anyone who possessed the proper personal virtues (initiative, perseverance, frugality, industry, reliability) could raise himself [or herself] from poverty to wealth." (Hearn 1977, 4) The farm and pioneer novels of the Twenties and Thirties repeatedly reaffirm the American dream of success. One literary critic labeled Edna Ferber's *So Big* (1924) as "another extended homily on the gospel of rugged individualism" (Stuckey 1966, 51), with protagonist Selina DeJong and young Roelf, the farm boy who grows up to become a famous sculptor, as examples of "rags-to-riches heroes and heroines who 'did it alone, in spite of everything.' " (Stuckey 1966, 52) Likewise, a score of fictional heroines in the interwar period, either by themselves or at their husbands' side, prove that fortune attends those who have the will and strength to seize it. Readers knew that fictional frontier men and women, like the heroes and heroines of fairy tales, had to demonstrate patience, courage, and determination in confronting a series of trials before achieving prosperity. In the novels of the period, no self-respecting fictional pioneer family can take pride in its achievements before it has survived one or more droughts, several blizzards, a severe fire, a plague of locusts, a wolf or panther attack, and perhaps an Indian raid. By the end of such novels, the heroes and heroines have achieved success entirely through their own efforts; they have tamed the wilderness and they have attained material prosperity.

Although Charles R. Hearn traces the American dream of success back to Puritan times in *The American Dream in the Great Depression* (1977), he finds that in the boom years of the Twenties "the cult of prosperity and the worship of success took on the proportions of a national religion." (24) Popular fiction and nonfiction writers generated vast quantities of success literature, and even the serious writers of the day were obsessed with the theme of success, although they presumably approached the issue with "greater depth and complexity" than did the popular writers of the decade. (52)

While one might expect that the Depression years would have prompted a widespread reappraisal of the validity of the doctrine of self-help, Hearn and other cultural historians have found this not to have been the case. Perhaps because frontier novelists repeatedly chronicled a rise from material deprivation to material abundance, their fiction continued to have wide circulation during the Thirties. Furthermore, as James Guimond has observed in *American Photography and the American Dream* (1991), the frontier version of the American myth of success was also popular in the history books and public murals of the period. (107) Likewise, according to John Bodnar in *Remaking America: Public Memory, Commemoration, and Patriotism in the Twentieth Century* (1992), Midwestern centennial town celebrations used pioneer imagery to "reaffirm the fact that difficult times had been overcome before." (127) Thus, in an effort to frame the hardships of the Depression present in a more positive context, historians, painters, and novelists drew upon images of pioneer life to suggest that the American spirit could not be dashed by adversity, that hard work and self-reliance were virtues that would eventually be rewarded by material success. Carroll's *As the Earth Turns*, a farm novel, was a Book-of-the-Month Club selection, ranked second on the best-seller list for 1933, and was made into a film by Warner Brothers in 1934. Bess Streeter Aldrich's pioneer novels were consistent best-sellers. For readers fearful of impending foreclosure on their mortgage, it may have been enjoyable to read about characters who were completely self-sufficient, for whom banks were nonexistent. For readers who were forced to cut back on expenditures for necessities and to curtail purchases of luxuries altogether, it may have made their personal hardships seem less severe when they read about characters who had few necessities and no luxuries at all. More significantly, like the murals and the histories of the day, these novels, too, encouraged Americans to regard their present difficulties as only temporary. "Historical themes," comments Karal Ann Marling in her study of post-office murals of the Thirties, "spoke to the issue of historical continuity." Mural viewers "looked forward confidently and hopefully to an America to come." (1982, 210) Furthermore, muralists and novelists alike encouraged their audiences to look to themselves for assistance in extricating themselves from a troubled time. As the Depression deepened, many readers may well have found stories of rural and frontier life increasingly inspirational. Again and again, the protagonists overcame formidable odds, combatting natural disasters and unyielding soil with the aid of nothing but their own determination and courage.

While most farm and pioneer novels of the interwar era emphasized themes of progress and success, authors were careful not to place too great a stress upon the accumulation of wealth and material goods for their own sake. Instead, writers portrayed farming heroes and heroines as characters who viewed their labor as a process valuable in itself—and as an avenue toward the achievement of more socially responsible ends than mere acquisition of money. In Bess Streeter Aldrich's *Spring Came on Forever* (1935), for example, Joe Holmsdorfer farms because he likes being a farmer, because "[w]ork was good . . . [and was] every man's portion in life." (264) When his materialistic and selfish wife Myrtie induces him to retire and move to a house in town, we are expected to regard Joe as a defeated man. Similarly, Gus Bragdon in Gladys Hasty Carroll's *A Few Foolish Ones* (1935) works hard because he loves his land, not because he wants to make a lot of money. True to the Protestant ethic, however, the fact that Bragdon does become prosperous is proof that he is capable and hardworking, that he is deserving of his good fortune. At the age of eighty, he sells most of his wood-lots for forty thousand dollars. "Not bad," Carroll informs us, "to have been dug by one pair of hands out of twenty acres of thin and rocky Maine soil. Not bad, what the Bragdons, yeoman farmers from the north of England, had accumulated since leaving the old country. The first Gus, looking ahead, had been satisfied. The last, looking back, was no less so. Workers, both of them." (355)

Many protagonists strive to improve their lot in order to provide their children with the opportunities they themselves have been forced to forego. Abbie Deal in Aldrich's *A Lantern in Her Hand* lives out her thwarted dreams in the lives of her children and grandchildren, while *So Big*'s Selina DeJong toils to give her son the chance to follow the career of his choice. In other cases, pioneers regard their efforts as a small but integral part of a greater endeavor to civilize the wilderness; they view themselves, as do Diony and Berk Jarvis in Elizabeth Madox Roberts' *The Great Meadow* (1930), as participants in a campaign to "start a new world" (110) and to "nurture a fine race, [in] a land of promise." (49)

It is clear that the authors of farm and pioneer novels do not hold with the notion that material success is desirable in and of itself. Twenties writers seem to be trying to combat an increasing public emphasis upon consumption facilitated by the growing prosperity of the decade. While F. Scott Fitzgerald questioned the value of wealth in *The Great Gatsby* and in such short stories as "A Diamond as Big as the Ritz," "The Ice Palace," and "The Rich Boy," and Sinclair Lewis attacked materialism head-on in *Babbitt*, farm and pioneer novelists criticized American consumption more subtly—by presenting portraits of families who made do on little and did not need to buy happiness. By the Thirties, as Americans' purchasing power declined drastically, novelists' depictions of farm and pioneer families who led full, contented lives beyond the reach of market forces helped readers to accept their own inability to buy the consumer items that they desired: if fictional rural families could be happy living at a subsistence level, then middle-class novel readers ought to be thankful for their comparative abundance.

In a number of farm and pioneer novels, families demonstrate their lack of a materialistic orientation by the manner in which they celebrate holidays, particularly Christmas. Given the fact that these books were written in an era in which Christmas was fast becoming the major shopping season of the year and a time during which children were coming to expect a wider array of more expensive presents than had past generations of youngsters, the depiction of a simpler and less commercialized holiday must have appealed to many readers. In Laura Ingalls Wilder's popular children's book *Little House in the Big Woods* (1932), for instance, the family lives in a log cabin in a remote region of Wisconsin far from any town or city. Thus, the family must make do with homemade gifts. The children awake on Christmas morning to find that they each have a pair of mittens and a piece of peppermint candy in their stockings. Laura is beside herself with delight when she discovers that she has also received a rag doll with a "face of white cloth with black button eyes," lips stained red with pokeberries, and curly hair of black yarn. (74)

Not only do farm and pioneer novels reaffirm the myth of success while indirectly criticizing the consumerist ethic; of perhaps greatest importance in our analysis of novels written by, about, and for women in this era, many of these books also represent a reaction against social changes occurring in this period. The farm and pioneer novels of the times permitted social conservatives to turn their backs upon a potentially troubling present and return to a "golden age" of gender relationships. In pioneer novels, this "golden age" is separated from the present by time, while in farm novels it is space which isolates the characters from the lives of a majority of the books' readers. While some women novelists use the farm and pioneer genres to introduce female protagonists whose actions redefine women's traditional place in society, more often women writers of farm and pioneer novels feature heroines who conform to conventional standards of female behavior, seldom questioning the gender roles which society has assigned them. Interestingly enough, both those women writers of the Twenties and Thirties who set out to demonstrate that women had the ability and strength to stand alone and those who attempted to show that women belonged in more subordinate roles relied on prototypes provided by Willa Cather.

In *O Pioneers!* (1913) Cather constructed one of the strongest woman characters yet to appear in American fiction. Alexandra Bergson, daughter of a Swedish immigrant who has struggled for eleven years to become a successful farmer on the Nebraska prairie, is left in charge of family and farm by her dying father. Alexandra proves to be worthy of her father's confidence. The next few years are hard, but, though many of the Bergsons' neighbors begin to despair of ever taming the land and her own brothers are ready to admit failure and sell out, Alexandra retains her faith in the prairie. Unlike male pioneers who perceive themselves to be fighting against the frontier, ruthlessly bending it to their will, Alexandra has a more empathetic relationship with her environment. Because Alexandra turns toward the land "with love and yearning," the prairie responds by bending "lower than it ever bent to a human will before." (65) Under Alexandra's hands, as Cather's section titles indicate, the "Wild Land" becomes "Neighboring Fields."[1]

Alexandra Bergson is certainly unlike most previous fictional heroines. One scholar has termed Alexandra a "paradigm of the autonomous woman," noting that both Alexandra and Thea Kronberg in Cather's *The Song of the Lark* (1915) are "female heroes, women not primarily defined by relationship to men, or children, but by commitment to their own destinies and their own sense of themselves." (Lambert 1982, 679) Although the novel ends with Alexandra's marriage, this event is hardly the climax of the story. Alexandra and Carl's union is a union of friends, not of lovers. Carl is aware that Alexandra's first love is still the land: " 'You belong to the land,' Carl murmured, 'as you have always said. Now more than ever.' " (307)

If Alexandra "belongs" to the land, Antonia Shimerda, the subject of Cather's other great pioneer novel, *My Antonia* (1918), "belongs" to other people. Even the narrator of the story of this Bohemian immigrant feels entitled to write about "my" Antonia. As a girl, she plows the fields, not because of her love for the land but because she takes pride in helping her family survive. As the Harlings' hired girl, the narrator tells us (with a tinge of jealousy), she is "fairly panting with eagerness to please" her employers' son Charlie. (155) As Cather scholar Susan Rosowski notes, "Antonia offers unconditional love: both her strength and her weakness is that 'I never could believe harm of anybody I loved.' " (1981, 266) Eventually Antonia marries fellow Bohemian Anton Cuzak. The two buy a farm and raise a large family, and Antonia lavishes her considerable store of love upon husband and children.

Narrator Jim Burden grew up with Antonia on the Nebraska prairie. When he leaves Nebraska to study law in New York, he realizes that it is Antonia's face that he means "always to carry with me; the closest, realest face, under all the shadows of women's faces, at the very bottom of my memory." (322) Antonia has become all women to Jim. By the time Jim finally returns to the prairie and to Antonia, twenty years have passed. On the first night of his visit to Antonia and her family, Jim lies awake on his blankets in the barn, thinking of Antonia. It is her ability to bring forth life that impresses Jim:

She had only to stand in the orchard, to put her hand on a little crab tree and look up at the apples, to make you feel the goodness of planting and tending and harvesting at last. All the strong things of her heart came out in her body, that had been so tireless in serving generous emotions.

It was no wonder that her sons stood tall and straight. She was a rich mine of life, like the founders of early races. (353)

While Alexandra is a strong and independent goddess of the land, Antonia is a mother-figure, who brings forth a race of pioneers to till the soil. Many later novelists, as we shall see, will model their heroines on one of these two prototypes, sometimes emphasizing the competence and self-reliance of their protagonists and sometimes stressing their fecundity and maternal devotion.

Ellen Glasgow and Edna Ferber, both of whom published farm novels in the mid-1920s, featured central characters much like Alexandra Bergson. Glasgow's *Barren Ground* was published in 1925, when the fifty-two-year-old Southern writer was nearing the height of her career. *Barren Ground* is set in contemporary rural Virginia. Dorinda Oakley's father is "land poor": he owns more acreage than he can cultivate and obstinately plants corn year after year, thereby exhausting the soil and steadily decreasing his yield.When Joshua dies, Dorinda takes over the farm. She buys dairy cows, uses modern farming techniques, and becomes the most successful farmer in the region.

Dorinda, like Alexandra, has a spiritual affinity with the land. Under Dorinda's care, the long-neglected and impoverished fields on her father's farm are restored to their original fertility, just as Alexandra converts virgin prairie to well-tended and high-yielding farmland. Both Dorinda and Alexandra find it easier to relate to the soil than to the human beings around them. "To the land," Glasgow writes, Dorinda "had given her mind and heart with the abandonment that she had found disastrous in any human relation." (365) Similarly, Alexandra's mind is a "white book, with clear writing about weather and beasts and growing things" (Cather 1913, 205)—and with little about people and their ways. Yet, as these passages indicate, Dorinda's closeness to the land is a bitter, almost involuntary retreat from the trauma of rejection by her lover—unlike Alexandra's more instinctive, joyous, and voluntary embrace of the world of nature. It was Dorinda's investing the weak and undependable Jason Greylock with the qualities of a romantic hero that led to her disillusionment; Alexandra, on the other hand, has simply been too busy farming to have "indulged in sentimental reveries." (Cather 1913, 205) Dorinda accepts the role of victim for which it appears that fate has cast her, while Alexandra writes her own story and casts herself.

Dorinda Oakley differs from Alexandra Bergson in that Dorinda reacts to circumstances while Alexandra rises above her vississitudes. On the other hand, the heroine of Edna Ferber's *So Big* (1924) is like Alexandra in that she, too, is mistress of her destiny. Written by a Midwesterner known prior to the publication of *So Big* primarily for her popular magazine stories featuring traveling saleswoman Emma McChesney, *So Big* was Edna Ferber's first best seller. Awarded the Pulitzer Prize for 1925 and made into a film by Warner Brothers in 1932, *So Big* made Ferber's reputation as a popular novelist, a reputation quickly augmented by the subsequent successes of *Show Boat* (1926), which was made into a film, a play, and a radio program; and *Cimarron* (1929), a Western dealing with the opening of the Oklahoma territory.

In *So Big*, as in *Barren Ground* and *O Pioneers!*, the heroine proves to be a better farmer than the male head of household has been. When her father dies, young Selina must make her own living. She becomes a teacher in a Dutch school in High Prairie, a truck farming district southwest of Chicago. Less than a year after her arrival in High Prairie, Selina marries Pervus DeJong and becomes a farmer's wife. Brighter and better educated than her husband, she sees his limitations plainly. She realizes that their "little farm was mismanaged through lack of foresight, imagination, and— she faced it squarely—through stupidity. She was fond of this great, kindly, blundering, stubborn boy who was her husband. But she saw him with amazing clearness through the mists of love." (130) She sends away for books on agriculture and tries to get her husband to change his ways, but he tells her that what was good enough for his father is good enough for him.

Daunted but not discouraged, Selina sets out to persuade Pervus to modernize the farm. She has effected only modest improvements when he dies, leaving her with a failing farm and a nine-year-old son. Selina courageously perceives this turn of events as merely a temporary reversal of fortune in the "great adventure" of life (109) and promptly undertakes to manage the farm alone. Over the next six years, through hard work and the aid of a loan from the father of an old school friend, Selina "changed the

DeJong acres from a worn-out and down-at-the-heel truck farm whose scant products brought a second-rate price in a second-rate market to a prosperous and blooming vegetable garden whose output was sought a year in advance by the South Water Street commission merchants." (217)

O Pioneers!, *Barren Ground*, and *So Big* all present heroines whose competence is underscored by the lack of ability exhibited by the significant male characters in these novels. Propelled into positions of responsibility by the usual means by which women of the era gained authority— through the death of the male head of household—all three of these female protagonists proceed to demonstrate their superiority in business acumen and farming instincts over the males whom they replace. All three writers have produced works which loosely conform to what would become the standard plot for pioneer novels. Through hard work and intelligent management, Alexandra Bergsen, Dorinda Oakley, and Selina DeJong survive and prosper. Success is shown to be the reward of those who possess sufficient determination and self-reliance to attain it. These characters all underscore the point that such traits are not exclusively the property of male protagonists. In an era in which women were gaining confidence in their ability to succeed in what had long been considered a man's world, these heroines served as proof that women were men's equals in overcoming both natural and human obstacles—that sometimes women were even men's superiors in this regard.[2]

One of the reasons why Alexandra Bergson has become prosperous by the end of *O Pioneers!*, Antonia and her husband Anton Cuzak have "got through" the hard times of their early years on the farm in *My Antonia*, and Selina DeJong manages to succeed with her truck farm is that all of these characters have been strengthened by the harsh conditions of pioneer life. The weaker characters in these novels are those who have forgotten—or who have never known—tribulation. As Robert Thacker remarks in *The Great Prairie Fact and Literary Imagination* (1989), Cather wrote her pioneer novels after the era of the frontier had ended and she "knew well of the smug materialists who succeeded the pioneering generation. Indeed, she satirizes their lack of imagination and taste through Alexandra's brothers, grown affluent by her foresight." (146) This theme is more fully developed in *So Big*, in which Selina struggles to give her son Dirk the advantages she never had. With the farm's profits, she sends him to college in Chicago and then to architecture school in the East. Despite his mother's influence, Dirk matures into a weaker-willed individual than Selina. Dirk is unable to throw himself into the pursuit of any goal with the resolution and enthusiasm that Selina has committed to the improvement of the DeJong acres. Although he rises to an important—and well-paying—position in banking, he eventually realizes that he is not the man his mother would have wished him to be. The point is brought forcibly home to him when Dallas O'Mara, the woman he loves, rejects his marriage proposal, telling him that he does not have enough character. She remarks that

"you haven't got a mark on you. Not a mark. You quit being an architect, or whatever it was, because architecture was an uphill disheartening job . . . if you had kept on—if you had loved it enough to keep on—fighting and struggling, and sticking it out—why, that fight would show in your face to-day. . . . Listen. I'm not criticizing you. But you're all smooth. I like 'em bumpy." (Ferber 1924, 348)

Dirk looks down at his smooth hands and thinks of another pair of hands— his mother's, "with the knuckles enlarged, the skin broken—expressive— her life written on them. Scars. She had them." (Ferber 1924, 348) Ferber, thus, reverses standard gender stereotypes: here, it is the man who is soft and the woman who is tough.

Bess Streeter Aldrich is another writer who frequently and forcefully suggests that the crucible of wilderness life produces strong, self-reliant women, while the easier existence of the settled prairie yields more materialistic, weaker, and more frivolous individuals. Yet, in Aldrich's case, her heroines serve to reinforce existing gender stereotypes rather than to undercut them. The granddaughter of pioneer families who journeyed to the Iowa frontier by oxcart in the 1850s and the daughter of parents who married in a log cabin in 1855, Bess Streeter Aldrich celebrates the pioneer spirit in her novels. Born in 1881, Aldrich did not experience frontier life herself, but, she later wrote, from "early association with many relatives who did live through the settling of the Midwest, I gained much first-hand information concerning that period and have made use of it in many books." (Kunitz and Haycraft 1942, 16)

Aldrich wrote *A Lantern in Her Hand* (1928) as a "tribute to the pioneer mother." (Kunitz and Haycraft 1942, 16) Abbie MacKenzie Deal, the protagonist of the novel, is not a heroine with the independence of an Alexandra Bergson; rather, Abbie is a character constructed along the lines of Antonia Cuzak, a devoted wife and mother who is matriarch of a new race of prairie-inhabitants. Unlike Cather's Antonia, however, who no more duplicates traditional images of Western women than does Alexandra Bergson, Aldrich's Abbie Deal closely conforms to what Sandra L. Myres in *Westering Women and the Frontier Experience, 1800–1915* (1982) identifies as one of the most commonly held stereotypes of frontierswomen. Abbie is the "sturdy helpmate and civilizer of the frontier." As Myres describes her, such a woman was "reluctant to go West, but once the decision was made, she trod westward with grim-faced determination. . . baby at breast, rifle at the ready, bravely awaited unknown dangers, and dedicated herself to removing wilderness from both man and land and restoring civilization as rapidly as possible." (2) Thus, Abbie is aghast when her young husband Will announces soon after the birth of their first child that they are leaving Iowa for Nebraska. As "sturdy helpmate" of her husband, Abbie may be unhappy at the prospect of leaving friends and family, but she nevertheless does not dispute her husband's decision. The story takes place, according to Aldrich, prior to the "era of freedom"; consequently, only one course of action is open to Abbie. "Abbie Deal's man had said he was going to Nebraska, and Abbie had to go too. It was as simple as that, then."(Aldrich 1928, 62) Abbie may be hesitant to migrate West, but her love for Will gives her the courage to face the unknown: "If being with Will meant making a new home in a far, unsettled country, why, then, she chose to journey bravely to the far, unsettled country." (Aldrich 1928, 65)

Is Aldrich's fictional account consistent here with the experience of actual pioneer women? Were real nineteenth-century women reluctant to migrate West? The surviving evidence is contradictory.[3] Whether or not most actual pioneer women wanted to venture Westward, however, most fictional frontiers women clearly are not eager to do so. Like Abbie Deal, the protagonists in women's pioneer novels are unwilling to leave their familiar surroundings and are propelled to do so only because of their love for and loyalty to their husbands. As these novels were being written at a time during which many middle-class women were beginning to demand a more equal role in family decision making, it seems clear that, whatever the historical record might show, popular women novelists with a conservative agenda with regard to a woman's place in society readily presented pioneer heroines who dutifully followed their husbands West despite their personal inclination to stay in the land of their youth.[4]

Once settled on the prairie, conditions, predictably, are hard. Abbie's family lives in a sod house, and after a cold and windy winter Abbie bears a second child. With the coming of spring, her spirits rise, and she "went happily about her work, one baby in her arms and the other at her skirts, courage her lode-star and love her guide." (Aldrich 1928, 84) Abbie needs all of her courage and love to cope with a seemingly endless series of crises: bad weather, crop failure, a plague of locusts, the death of a son in childbirth. Through it all, Abbie is content. She is beside the man she loves, and, "a born mother" (125), she has, eventually, four healthy children. And she is working to realize a vision of the future. Aldrich invests Will with the ability to see the larger picture: he looks toward the time when the wilderness will be transformed into a settled landscape of cultivated farmland, scattered villages, and great cities. Inspired by Will's vision, Abbie strives to achieve it within the domestic sphere. Exercising her "woman's prerogative" (137), she begins planning a frame house to replace their soddie, with a white picket fence to protect her flower garden.[5]

Having tamed the wilderness on the home front, Abbie makes a broader contribution toward the civilizing of the West through her children. As Abbie tells her granddaughter, she has dreamed her dreams and "the children are carrying them out." (279) When the children have grown to adulthood and bring their spouses back to the old home place for Christmas, there sit around the coal stove "the state legislator and the banker, the artist, the singer, and the college teacher. And in their midst, rocking and smiling, sat the little old lady who had brought them up with a song upon her lips and a lantern in her hand." (267)[6]

Like Cather and Ferber, Bess Streeter Aldrich suggests that the pioneer generation of women are the models against which all later generations must measure themselves. Unlike these earlier writers, however, Aldrich uses her heroines to achieve explicitly conservative ends. Her books, like the public murals of the Thirties, "celebrate intrepid pioneer women and yet uphold female dependency and maternity as the ultimate goals, to be achieved once the rigors of the frontier yield to a more settled life." (Melosh 1991, 47) In her forties during the 1920s, Aldrich appears to have been unsympathetic to the efforts of young women of the decade to redefine their social roles and revise traditional notions of what was considered appropriate with regard to women's goals and expectations. Reviewers of her books pointed to Aldrich's tendency to reaffirm traditional values in an era in which such values were under attack. As a *New York Times* reviewer wrote of Aldrich's *Miss Bishop* (1933), "In these days, when the reader of fiction is swimming in a sea of selfish heroines loudly declaring that they must express themselves, or that they have a right to happiness, it is refreshing to meet Miss Bishop." (*New York Times*, October 15,1933, 19) Likewise, the *Christian Century* commented of *White Bird Flying* (1931), another Aldrich novel, that it "gives one renewed faith in the fine old simplicities of life." (*Christian Century*, September 23, 1931, 1179)

In *A Lantern in Her Hand*, Aldrich presents Abbie Deal as being stronger and wiser than any of her offspring. Aldrich juxtaposes Abbie's outlook on life with those of her three daughters, using the contrast to criticize contemporary attitudes which she regards as misguided. Her daughter Isabelle tells Abbie that she and her husband have decided to remain childless so that they can devote their lives to art. " 'To have children,' Isabelle informs her mother, 'you ought to have plenty of time and money for their development' " (206), oblivious to the fact that Abbie and Will had neither time nor money when Isabelle and her siblings were young. Abbie thinks back to her years in the sod house and remembers that the "mother there was hearing reading lessons while she kneaded bread, was teaching songs while she scrubbed . . . was instilling into childish minds, ideals of honesty and clean living with every humble task." (206) While the modern reader finds it difficult to believe that any mother could be as accomplished, efficient, and—apparently—unruffled as Aldrich portrays Abbie to be, there is little question that the author is serious in presenting Abbie as a female model to be emulated. John's wife Eloise plans to take a different tack toward parenting: she and her husband will have children, but they will rear them in a "businesslike, systematic way." (212) Eloise raises her first child "by the ritual of a red volume in which she held implicit and humorless faith." (217) Abbie is visiting one day when the baby starts to cry. While Eloise consults the childcare manual, Abbie more practically examines the baby—and finds a safety pin sticking into him. By this incident, Aldrich none too subtly implies that reliance upon expert advice rather than upon experience and common sense in raising children is foolishness. A third child, Grace, informs her mother that she does not plan to marry at all. She means to be "free and independent," to pursue research work in the East, and she does not want to have to tailor her ambitions to accommodate the demands of husband or family. (236) Directly attacking the feminists' choice of career over marriage, Aldrich presents Grace's decision as being as wrongheaded as those of her sisters.

Abbie is troubled by her children's decisions and we, the readers, are meant to be troubled as well. In *A Lantern in Her Hand*, Bess Streeter Aldrich seems to have been trying to reemphasize a traditional image of woman-hood, to undo the changes which had occurred in the postwar period in women's perceptions of their roles and in their aspirations for the future. An old-fashioned woman, Abbie MacKenzie Deal's life is centered upon her husband and her children. She would never think of pursuing a "career," limiting her family, or raising her children with the aid of a reference book. Compared to Abbie's seeming naturalness, her children's attitudes seem curious, mistaken, even unnatural.

Paradoxically, while Aldrich frequently writes off the pioneers' children as too misguided and spineless to amount to much, she often treats the granddaughters more sympathetically. Brought up as "modern" misses, these young women gradually come to embrace the values and ways of their grandmothers. Despite the fact that this third generation has had even less contact with the frontier than their mothers, who at least spent their childhood on the untamed prairie, the granddaughters' will is not sapped nor their good judgment lost in the process of growing up in a less-challenging era. Somehow the younger women manage to overcome the disadvantages of their environment and prove themselves to be the true descendants of their pioneer foremother.

Succeeding generations of women are clearly contrasted, for example, in Aldrich's *Spring Came on Forever* (1935). Having come to maturity in the Twenties, Hazel Meier is quick to pick up the manners and morals of her coed peers: by "her junior year she was sophisticated, svelte, unruffled under any situation, told the house mother in velvet-concealed words where to get off, removed the velvet shield on occasion when some good sister crossed her path in social territory." (259) While still in college, Hazel promises to marry Neal, the great-grandson of Amalia Holmsdorfer, a member of the German pioneer community which settled the Nebraska territories. A year after their graduation, Hazel breaks off the engagement when Neal tells her that, because of his father's losses in the Depression, he is going to give up his plans to become a lawyer to stay home and manage the family farm. It is not until Neal rescues her from a floating roof during a flood that Hazel finally comes to understand that love is more important than social standing—or than personal independence. Hazel marries Neal, and, significantly, takes up housekeeping on the very land where Amalia had homesteaded years before. "Peculiarly," Aldrich tells us, "in spite of the difference in generations, Hazel approached her task much as the young Amalia had once done, vigorously and with responsibility." (322) In part, it is the crisis of the Depression, like the hard times of the pioneer era, which brings out the strength and determination inherent in the early settlers' granddaughters—and prompts them to lay aside their "misguided" notions of female independence to assume their "rightful" places as helpmates to their husbands.

If Bess Streeter Aldrich combats what she sees as the pernicious impact of contemporary notions upon the behavior and values of young women by introducing present-generation female characters who come to recognize the error of their ways and adopt the ideology of their grandmothers, Gladys Hasty Carroll takes a slightly different approach. In *As the Earth Turns* (1933) and *A Few Foolish Ones* (1935), Carroll features present-day rural protagonists who unquestioningly accept traditional notions as to a woman's proper sphere and who attack their household tasks with as much energy and skill as any frontierswoman struggling for survival on the prairie. In *As the Earth Turns* nineteen-year-old Jen Shaw has been mistress of her father's house ever since her mother's death ten years earlier. Jen is a model of housewifely competence: she cooks and bakes, cans and preserves, tends her gardens, darns clothing, and delivers a baby—all with equal deftness. Mr. Keele, a dry goods peddler who plies his wares throughout the Maine countryside and who has had plenty of opportunity for comparison, swears that "nobody could cook like Jen Shaw." (42) She is equally as capable with children, who "were no trouble to her; two or five or an even dozen, it was all the same." (199) When a Polish family moves nearby, it is Jen who hurries through the night to attend to a croupy infant. She doses the child with ipecac and presses wet hot towels on his neck and chest and is "not surprised that she had no help; not only Polish mothers stood aside to let her have her way with ailing babies." (101)

The Polish Stan Janowski, more imaginative than the stolid Anglo-Saxons among whom he finds himself, thinks of Jen Shaw as a goddess—"and finds no humor in the thought, though Jen was short and stocky with a broad, contented face." (328) If Jen is a goddess, she is a goddess of the hearth, as the center of Jen's world is her kitchen and her universe is the cluster of farms which comprise the rural neighborhood in which she lives. Attuned to the changes in the seasons and sensitive even to subtle variations in the weather, Jen conceives of social arrangements as part of nature as well. Accepting the notion that men and women occupy separate spheres, Jen "indulgently" overlooks Stan's seeming to recognize no gender boundaries, tolerantly attributing his aberrant thinking to his foreign upbringing.

Gladys Hasty Carroll's ideology is a conservative one, not only in her presentation of gender roles but also in economic philosophy. Although *As the Earth Turns* was published in 1933, at a time when farmers across the country were indeed in serious trouble due to the collapse of the international financial system and the failure of a decade of business-oriented presidential administrations to address agricultural needs, Carroll does not acknowledge the legitimacy of the farmers' criticisms. Instead, she speaks through the confident and prosperous Mark Shaw to discount his son George's censure of federal farm policy as the frustrated ranting of an ineffectual farmer whose failures should more properly be attributed to his own poor judgment than to a lack of government support. Jen's brother George is a querulous, ineffective farmer modeled loosely upon Alexandra Bergson's brother Lou in *O Pioneers!* Like Lou, George refuses to shoulder the blame for his own shortcomings. It is because of bad weather, George tries to tell his father, that he could not grow enough hay to feed his livestock over the winter, ignoring the older man's comment that "them that cut their hay when it was ripe last summer had enough to last them through." (134) When George contends it is because the government is not helping them out financially that farmers like himself are in trouble across the country, Mark Shaw is again unconvinced. "He did not doubt George was right that farmers should be helped, but he knew they never would be. There was no help but hard work and painstaking and strength and willingness. Without these a man was not a farmer." (134) The reader concludes that George has brought his problems upon himself. Carroll implies that government aid would only serve to prop up incompetent farmers like George, who perhaps deserve to fail because they lack initiative and common sense. This position indeed was held by many, at first to rationalize the Hoover administration's failure to act decisively with regard to the farm crisis and later to condemn New Deal agricultural relief measures.[7]

The authors of all of the novels we have thus far analyzed in this chapter depict protagonists who battle vigorously to overcome the hardships which beset them. In each case, the heroine's character is strengthened in the struggle and she succeeds in confronting the various crises with fortitude and competence. Two novels, however, reject the comfortable worldview affirmed in most women's farm and pioneer novels and feature female protagonists who differ markedly from the typical heroines of such books. Awarded the Pulitzer Prize for 1934 and 1935, respectively, Caroline Miller's *Lamb in His Bosom* (1933) and Josephine Johnson's *Now in November* (1934) present dark and troubling pictures of the plight of rural Americans—past and present.

Caroline Miller is the only woman writer under discussion who constructs a frontier heroine who seems buffeted by circumstance rather than in charge of her fate. While such an image is not uncommon in pioneer literature by male writers—Ole Rölvaag's characterization of Beret Hansa in *Giants in the Earth* or Hamlin Garland's portraits of his mother in his various autobiographies come most immediately to mind[8]—women novelists, as we have seen, have been much more likely to depict strong-minded and competent females who are equal to whatever predicaments in which they may find themselves. In contrast, Cean Carver, the protagonist of *Lamb in His Bosom* (1933), which is set on the Georgia frontier in the antebellum period, is weakened, not strengthened, by the hard life of the frontier.

Cean marries Lonzo Smith and moves with him to the backwoods of Georgia, where she settles into a routine of unremitting toil. In addition to performing the backbreaking round of household chores required of the pioneer woman—such as washing and boiling the clothes, churning the butter, helping with the seeding and the hoeing, and cooking over the open fire—Cean undergoes a seemingly endless succession of pregnancies. Before her childbearing years mercifully come to an end, she has had fourteen children. Scarcely an earth mother along the lines of Cather's Antonia Cuzek or Aldrich's Abbie Deal, Cean's pregnancies are painful and her children are demanding and quarrelsome. Not only is Cean forced to endure an onerous daily existence, but she must also confront a series of catastrophes. While she acts decisively to thwart disaster in some cases, in other instances she can do nothing to avert misfortune. Alone with two small daughters when she goes into labor with her first son, she is obliged to deliver the baby alone—and to shoot immediately afterward an attacking panther. Later in the book she is forced to watch helplessly as one of her daughters burns to death. Still later, her house burns down while her husband is away. By the end of the novel, Cean's physical appearance reflects the hard life she has led: Miller tells us that she "was bent and lean . . . her face was furrowed and her hair was thin and white and tightly drawn over her skull." (337) Although Cean has remarried and life is easier for her in her old age than it was when she was younger, Miller, unlike Edna Ferber or Bess Streeter Aldrich, gives the reader little indication that her characters have found that life is a great adventure or that hard work will eventually lead to prosperity.

Miller depicts a harsh world in which the woman's lot is only marginally harder than the man's. No one remonstrates with Cean's brother when he strikes his wife. Parents hope for sons, not daughters: fathers "would need boys to help break ground and pull fodder; girls were good for but little, except to weave and pick cotton." (79) Women are perpetually worn out by the bearing and raising of large families, in part because family planning is regarded as sinful by most members of Cean's society. Miller suggests that it is a patriarchal society which reinforces this belief: when Cean takes steps to postpone another pregnancy after the coming of her second child, she keeps her actions secret from her husband, as "he would never have forgiven her, and well she knew it." (143) Despite her empathy with the hardships of her women characters, Miller scarcely suggests that life for men is easy in frontier Georgia. The author neither condones nor attacks the gender roles and relationships of the period. Instead, the inescapable message of this relentlessly realistic book seems to be that times were hard in the backwoods a century ago for both men and women and that no amount of determination or effort and no reorganization of gender relationships could effect a substantial alleviation of the harshness of frontier conditions. If Cean is worn down by her experiences in the backwoods, so are the other characters—both males and females.

Life for Marget Haldmarne and her family in *Now in November* (1934), the first novel of its twenty-four-year-old author, is equally difficult. Farm novel *Now in November* no more offers platitudes to assure the reader that one can achieve success through intelligent hard work than does pioneer novel *Lamb in His Bosom*. In this respect, Josephine Johnson's book also resembles another Pulitzer Prize-winning farm novel of the Depression, John Steinbeck's *Grapes of Wrath* (1939). Even if Johnson ultimately rejects Steinbeck's notion that "[o]nly through a strong communal unity and class solidarity can the dispossessed hope to grasp their share" of land and opportunity (Hearn 1977, 88), she joins Steinbeck in repudiating the American belief in "privatized" social mobility through the honest toil of individual persons or families.

Now in November is a tale of unrequited love, insanity, suicide, drought, and death by fire; but contributing more substantively to its mood of despair is the characters' constant feeling of entrapment. Arnold Haldmarne, the narrator's father, left the family farm at sixteen to work in the lumber factories. With the onset of the Depression, Haldmarne is forced to confront the "strange blankness and dark of being neither wanted nor necessary any more." (6) In desperation, he returns with his wife and three daughters to the land the Haldmarne family has owned since the Civil War to take up farming. Unfortunately, Haldmarne must mortgage his property in order to obtain the capital to get started and,try as he might, he is never able to earn enough money to pay off his debts. In her very first days on the farm, Marget, the narrator, feels the "beginning of fear. Fear that life wasn't safe and comfortable, or even just tight and hard, but that there was an edge of darkness which was neither, and was something which no one could ever explain or understand." (24)

The tone of *Now in November* is in stark contrast to that of Gladys Hasty Carroll's *As the Earth Turns*, a more "mainstream" women's novel of the Depression era, which, as we have seen, is also an account of a contemporary farming family. Reviewers of Carroll's book had pointed to the Shaws'

"dignity and zest," (*Christian Science Monitor*, May 6, 1933, 8), and admired
the family's "courage and serenity," as qualities which "one seldom finds
in modern fiction" (*Forum*, June 1933, 89)—and they were certainly not
present in *Now in November*. Both *As the Earth Turns* and *Now in November*
follow the characters through a succession of seasons. This structure con-
tributes to the peacefulness and assurance of Carroll's novel: the world in
which the Shaws move is a world which constantly renews itself, which
dies only to be born again. As one reviewer commented, the novel "runs
smoothly and deeply in its seasonal rustic rhythm." (*Books*, May 7, 1933, 1)
No such tranquility results from Johnson's use of a seasonal structure. As
Marget herself asserts at one point: "I do not see in our lives any great ebb
and flow or rhythm of earth. There is nothing majestic in our living. The
earth turns in great movements, but we jerk about on its surface like gnats,
our days absorbed and overwhelmed by a mass of little things." (226) Even
in the novel's first section, set in springtime, the narrator's delight with the
miracle of reawakening is shadowed by the fear that this will be the year
in which her father will be unable to make his mortgage payments: "Not
even on April nights heavy with grape smell, or in the moving of shadow-
leaves could my mind forget the inevitable noon." (47) The promise of
spring is not realized in the summer, which becomes "The Long Drouth"
of the second section of the novel. Month follows month without rain, and
Johnson vividly details the consequences. The devastation of the external
landscape is mirrored by the narrator's interior desolation. Her love for
hired man Grant Koven, an emotion which was born in hope in the spring,
meets with only friendly indifference from Koven, and Marget becomes
increasingly despondent as the summer drags on. The season ends on a
dramatic note: Marget's older sister Kerrin slashes her wrists after hurling
a knife at her father; trapped in a fire, Mother is surrounded by the flames
and badly burned; and Koven, whose love for Marget's sister Merle is no
more reciprocated than Marget's love for him, leaves for good. By the time
the novel has moved to its third and last section, "Year's End," the reader
has the impression that the shift of seasons in *Now in November* is not a
cyclical movement but a linear progression. The book has moved inexorably from spring to winter, where it has reached its logical and permanent
conclusion. With Mother's death, we cannot conceive that there will ever
be a return of spring, with its renewal of life and hope.[9]

In *As the Earth Turns*, Carroll depicts Jen Shaw as the image of competence and self-assurance: like her father Mark, she never gets tired, loses
her temper, or makes a mistake. She accepts without question the traditional gender division of labor, automatically rejecting her suitor Stan
Janowski's offer to help with the dishes. Johnson's characters are neither so
effortlessly capable and confident nor so bound by conventional gender
roles. While Johnson portrays Mother as having an inner peace supported
by her abiding "faith in the dignity of the human spirit" (145), even

Mother's faith is shaken by the reverses the Haldmarne family must weather. Kerrin is as competent as a man at farm tasks; she is impatient with Father's failure to succeed at farming and would probably make a better farmer than he. Yet, as Kerrin slides into insanity, she become incapable of performing even the simplest of jobs. Father may believe that only men have any business managing a farm, but, at the end of the novel, Marget sees that Father has aged and accepts that she and Merle will have to take over his tasks when he can no longer carry them out. While the death of the male heads of household in Ferber's *So Big* and Glasgow's *Barren Ground* permits the heroines to prove that they are better farmers than their male predecessors, Arnold Haldmarne's decline appears to lead to no such outcome. Merle and Marget will be as buffeted by the implacable forces of nature and the marketplace as their father has been. Fear of failure will continue to shadow their future as it has their past.

By the end of *Now in November*, Marget concludes that she can rely upon nothing and no one for relief or succor, and she has little hope of better days ahead. She sees that hard work is of no avail in an economy in which farm prices are controlled by those with little concern for the plight of the farmer—and in an environment in which the vagaries of nature can be neither predicted nor avoided. She cannot depend on love—as it is not returned. She cannot trust in faith—what little faith she had has died with her mother. She sees that she cannot place confidence in human kindness— the townspeople and government officials have no sympathy for the farmers' predicament. Even nature cannot provide security, as it is "something both treacherous and kind, which could be trusted only to be inconstant, and would go its own way as though we were never born." (8–9) Ultimately, she loses hope in herself as well. She comes to realize that, if the "world [is] against us . . . we [are also] against ourselves." (227)[10]

Neither Caroline Miller's unsentimental account of pioneer life in the backcountry of Georgia in *Lamb in His Bosom* nor Josephine Johnson's dark narrative of a Missouri family's struggle to evade financial ruin during the Depression in *Now in November* fits the standard pattern of frontier or farm novels by women authors of the period. Present in embryo form in Cather's pioneer novels of the 'teens and developed into a fictional formula in the following decades, the structure of the farm and pioneer novel privileged a conservative reading of women's roles and expectations, reaffirmed the long-standing American belief in social mobility and individualism, and sought, first, to temper a decade's infatuation with materialism and, later, to provide fictional evidence that one need not be prosperous to achieve love and happiness—as one could reasonably expect to better one's conditions by and by. By the end of the Thirties, this genre did not so much subvert itself—Miller's and Johnson's novels remained exceptions to the rule, rather than becoming harbingers of a new direction in such fiction—as die out altogether. By the 1940s, farm and pioneer novels had virtually disappeared from the bookshops. Nevertheless, this change in publishing trends did not indicate the disappearance of the themes which had become common to such novels. From Zane Grey in the 'teens and Twenties to Louis L'Amour in the Seventies and Eighties, dozens of male writers had established the Western as a separate fictional type, sharing the emphasis upon individualism to be found in the farm and pioneer novel—albeit, with less emphasis upon social mobility. By the 1950s, a number of female writers had perfected the formulaic conventions of the romance novel, a genre which reflected the conservative ideology regarding gender roles which had been espoused in the 1920s and 1930s by many popular women novelists—including the authors of rural and pioneer fiction.

CHAPTER SIX

Sacrificial Heroines

A s we have seen, popular women writers frequently contrast their heroines with a variety of female secondary characters who do not possess the protagonists' virtues. The fictional heroines of the Twenties and Thirties do not serve—and are not intended by their creators to serve—as role models in the strictest sense of the term; their behavior is not purposely displayed to encourage the readers' emulation. The authors do not explicitly draw a didactic connection between virtue and happiness, between moral weakness and ruin, as did novelists of the eighteenth and early nineteenth centuries. Nevertheless, in most popular women's novels of the period, the heroine is rewarded for her goodness, while her foil—unless she repents and changes her ways—can expect only discontent. In novels which focus upon young unmarried protagonists, such as those by Kathleen Norris, Temple Bailey, and Gene Stratton-Porter, we have seen that the typical heroine is young, unassuming, and artless, while her rival is older, calculating, and sophisticated. In novels depicting married women, the typical protagonist is one who conforms to the code of domesticity, who is a natural-born wife and mother; the typical villainess, on the other hand, is a lazy and irresponsible housewife, an unwilling mother, and an ill-tempered wife. The heroine does not consider divorce, no matter how unsatisfactory her marriage may be; her foil has no such inhibitions; she ends her own marriage when it is convenient for her to do so, and she does not hesitate to threaten another woman's marriage by flirting with her husband. Given these patterns in the depiction of heroines and their foils, what conclusions may we draw regarding the essential characteristics society deemed most desirable in women in the Twenties and Thirties? In what ways are the popular women novelists of the era responding to, and helping shape, contemporary expectations of women?

According to Leslie Fiedler, who asserts in *Love and Death in the American Novel* (1966) that (male) American novelists from Cooper to Henry James divided their female characters into two types, the Fair Maiden and the Dark Lady, the basic difference between the heroine and her foil lay in the realm of sexual experience and passion. The Fair Maiden was pure and passionless, while the Dark Lady was the "sinister embodiment of the sexuality denied the snow maiden." (296) If such twentieth-century male novelists as Fitzgerald, Hemingway, and Faulkner, in Fiedler's opinion, reversed and collapsed the distinctions between the two character types, popular writers—both male and, as we have seen, female—continued to people their novels with good and bad women, and to distinguish clearly between the two. But, as the moral absolutes of the Victorian era weakened, sexual passion no longer marked off the bad woman from the good one in popular culture, as "good" women were acknowledged to have sexual drives, too. As Sumiko Higashi remarks of the portrayal of women on film, "The essence then of the changing screen image of women during the 'teens and Twenties was her maturation into a sexual being." (1978, 169) In popular fiction of the twentieth century, according to Kay Mussell in *Fantasy and Reconciliation: Contemporary Formulas of Women's Romance Fiction* (1984), what separates heroines from antiheroines is the heroines' ability to "express their sexual impulses at the right time and with the proper mate." (90) Unlike the heroine, the "Other Woman" is only too likely to crave sexual gratification without offering love in return. For example, the "vampire temptress," a female type Donald Makosky finds common in magazine short stories in the 'teens and Twenties, yields to "her desire to possess men [which] is never motivated by love, or self-giving, but always by the drive for more personal pleasure or power." (1966, 169)

Once a character's sexuality is replaced by her attitude toward others as a marker of her "goodness," then her motivations become as important as her actions in determining her moral worth. A heroine is self-sacrificing; a villainess is self-seeking. In their study of the fiction published in *Ladies' Home Journal* in 1905, Patricia Searles and Janet Mickish found that the short stories repeatedly assert that "it is important for women to submerge their identities and sacrifice themselves for others." (1984, 264) Three-quarters of a century later, heroines were still identified by their unselfishness in the romance fiction of the 1970s and 1980s. According to Mussell, "[s]uccess comes to women who possess the innate traits of good women—sexual control, modesty, intuition, selflessness, caring—but who use those qualities actively to benefit others." (1984, 90) These observations are equally applicable in describing the popular heroines of the Twenties and Thirties.

How is the heroine's selflessness to be recognized? Not by agitating for world peace, devoting her life to medicine, or donating her savings to charity. She demonstrates her unselfishness by wholeheartedly conforming to traditional notions of womanly behavior: she becomes a devoted wife and mother. The anti-heroine, on the other hand, not only does a poor job of carrying out her own family responsibilities, she also endangers the security of other women's families through her selfish desire for sexual satisfaction at any cost. As Bridget Fowler notes in her analysis of women's magazine fiction in Britain in the 1930s, villainesses "invariably lack all values except that of sensual experience and possess passions which threaten all established, ordered domestic structures." (1984, 121)

In popular women's novels of the Twenties and Thirties, a female character's moral worth can immediately be measured by the amount of attention which she gives to her physical appearance. In an era in which standards of beauty were increasingly set by advertisers and in which comeliness could be achieved through the judicious purchase of cosmetics, clothing, and accessories, popular women novelists decried what they deemed an excessive self-absorption fostered by a consumerist ethic. These writers published their books in a period in which a seemingly inordinate amount of time—as well as money—was devoted to the effort to achieve an ideal feminine appearance. As Lois W. Banner has noted in her survey of the history of beauty practices in the United States, the number of beauty parlors in the United States jumped from five thousand in 1920 to forty thousand a decade later. The cosmetics industry expanded as well, generating a sales volume of nearly $180 million by 1930. (1983, 271–72) More and more women may have been buying rouge sticks and powder puffs and regularly frequenting beauty parlors to have their hair bobbed and waved and their hands manicured, but their actions are reflected in the behavior of fictional antiheroines, not in the habits of the heroines. In most popular women's novels of the period, the heroine appears to give no thought to her appearance, while the antiheroine is excessively self-absorbed, painstakingly enhancing her less-than-perfect physical attributes with the aid of a battery of beauty products. When forty-one-year-old Isabelle Carter calls governess Harriet Field to her room in Kathleen Norris' *Harriet and the Piper* (1920), the younger woman notices that her employer's "lower eyelids had been skillfully darkened, her cheeks delicately rouged, and her lips touched with carmine; her brows had been clipped and trained and pencilled, her lashes brushed with liquid dye, and what fragrant powders and perfumes could add, had been added in generous measure." (33) Equally determined to reconstruct her appearance with the aid of beauty products is Adelaide Laramore, in Temple Bailey's *The Dim Lantern* (1923). When heroine Jane Barnes accepts the attentions of wealthy Frederick Towne, she finds Towne's previous girlfriend unwilling to relinquish her hold on him. Adelaide Laramore is nearly forty—almost twice Jane's age. In contrast to Jane's natural beauty, Adelaide's is artificially produced: "[s]he had a long face, with pink cheeks and pencilled eyebrows. She was like a portrait on porcelain, and she knew it, and emphasized the effect." (64)

While novelists like Kathleen Norris and Temple Bailey appear to denounce the notion of beauty as a consumer product, one doubts that this was precisely the message received by their readers. While the heroines may have disregarded their looks—as they could afford to do so, given that they were "naturally" beautiful—the authors, nonetheless, reinforce the importance of appearance. Female readers could hope to duplicate the heroines' wavy hair, clear skin, and dark lashes only through artificial means. By judicious application of beauty products, those whom nature had not endowed with "natural" beauty could appear to be authentically beautiful themselves. As Banner notes, this emphasis upon achieving a "natural" look was stressed both by cosmetics advertisers and by beauty parlor owners in the pre–World War I era. Thus, the natural look was not inconsistent with the use of beauty products. In the Twenties, as Paula Fass observes in her study of college students of that decade, young women used cosmetics not to enhance "natural" beauty but to emphasize artifice, "to draw attention to their use." (1977, 283) Nevertheless, Twenties cosmetics advertisers still exorted women to use their products in order to achieve a natural look of beauty. In the May 1926 issue of *Ladies' Home Journal*, for example, copywriters for Pompeian Beauty Powder claimed that "[a]ll smart women strive for a natural complexion" while the advertisers of Palmolive Soap asserted that "[t]o be charming today, one strives for natural beauty." Even though a nail polish advertisement in the same issue announced that, "for a newer, more exotic effect [consumers could try] the new Deep Rose Cutex Liquid Polish," *Journal* readers also learned that the polish was also available in "natural pink." Given the advertisers' own emphasis upon the achievement of "natural charm," it is not altogether clear whether women novelists like Bailey and Norris were opposed to all attempts to improve one's appearance with the aid of beauty products—or whether they were against only those efforts which called attention to themselves.[1]

Bailey and Norris not only suggest that "natural" beauty is all-important; they also imply that only the young can be beautiful. Here again, their position both reinforces and contradicts that of the advertisers of cosmetics and hair care products. From the turn of the century on, Banner notes, "the commercial beauty culture played a powerful role in standardizing the connection between beauty and youth." (1983, 225) Due at least in part to the advertising campaign mounted by the beauty industry, the Twenties marked the blossoming of the "new American cult of youth," when being young was a mark of beauty in itself. (Leuchtenburg 1958, 173) Thus, in Norris and Bailey novels, only the young are beautiful. Where Norris and Bailey depart from the advertisers, however, is in these writers' belief that once youth is gone it is fruitless to try to bring it back. While popular novelists like Norris and Bailey expressed disapproval of older women who attempt to recover their youth by artificial means, advertisers promised that use of their products would help a woman preserve her youthful appearance, "to catch and hold the springtime of her beauty." (Marchand 1985, 176) Well before the 1920s, cosmetics manufacturers had begun to feature beauty products which would hide the ravages of time or, better yet, retard them. By the Twenties, the claim that a given beauty product would restore the user's youthful looks had become commonplace in magazine advertisements.

Bailey and Norris are not the only best-selling women novelists to feature middle-aged female characters who attempt to simulate youth. In one popular novel of the Twenties, Gertrude Atherton's *Black Oxen* (1923), the fifty-nine-year-old protagonist goes so far as to undergo a glandular operation to reverse the aging process, becoming once again the belle she had been in her youth. While Atherton neither praises nor condemns Mary Zattiany for her action, few other popular women novelists of the era approve of characters who tamper with nature. Edith Wharton satirizes middle-aged women who attempt to preserve their youthfulness in *Twilight Sleep* (1927). Pauline Manford religiously does her eurythmic exercises and her gymnastics; she engages in mental deep-breathing and meditation; she submits to manicures and massages; she contemplates a face-lift; she attempts to insulate herself from life within an artificial cocoon of tranquility. In the end, none of these stratagems works. Try as she may, she cannot avoid the tell-tale wrinkles of age which result from her inability to avoid confronting painful truths about her family. "What was the use," she wonders unhappily, "of all the months and years of patient Taylorized effort against the natural human fate: against anxiety, sorrow, old age—if their menace was to reappear whenever events slipped from her control?" (114)

While there is nothing wrong with treasuring one's youthfulness while it lasts, once youth is gone, Wharton implies in what is essentially a repudiation of contemporary advertisers' advice to consumers, it is preferable to show one's age than to hide it. In *The Brimming Cup* (1921), Dorothy Canfield rejects both the notion that youth can be recovered once it is gone and the idea that it is more desirable to be youthful than to be middle-aged. In this novel, Canfield suggests that physical signs of aging are badges of experience. Former schoolmates Marise Crittenden and Eugenia Mills are both entering middle age. Marise takes life as it comes, regardless of its effect upon her appearance. Eugenia, who has arrived for her yearly visit with the Crittendens, disapprovingly observes that "as to wrinkles, of course a woman as unrestrained as Marise was bound to get them early. She had never learned the ABC of woman's wisdom, the steady cult of self-care, self-beautifying, self-refining." (260) Eugenia, on the other hand, attempts to avoid stress in order to preserve her youth: "horrified and alarmed to see deep lines of thought, of hope, of impatience, of emotion, criss-crossing fatally on her face" (256), she, like Wharton's Pauline Manford, resolutely sets herself to clearing her mind of all thoughts and feelings, hoping thereby to erase all trace of wrinkles. Having long been secretly infatuated with Marise's husband Neale, Eugenia hopes that Neale will finally come to see that she is more youthful-looking than his wife and will therefore transfer his affections from Marise to her. Such a notion, obviously, conforms to the message presented in advertisements of the day: then, as now, advertisers assured consumers that women who preserved their youth through the purchase and application of beauty products would attract men's attention. As Neale shows no signs of fulfilling this expectation, Eugenia ends her visit with the Crittendens. After Eugenia has gone, Neale remarks to Marise that Eugenia is "beginning to show her age." Marise suggests that this is a strange remark for him to make, "the husband of such a frankly middle-aged thing as I." When Neale has thought this over, he fastens upon what he sees as the essential difference between Eugenia and Marise: "you'll always look younger than she. No, not younger, that's not it, at all. It's *living*, you look. I tell you what, she's a cut flower in a vase, that's beginning to wilt, and you're a living plant." (389)

In Canfield's *The Brimming Cup*, as in Norris' *Harriet and the Piper* and Bailey's *The Dim Lantern*, the antiheroine's artificiality of appearance, her obsessive attention to her looks, signal an attitude toward life quite different from the heroine's. The heroine is compassionate and loving; she lives for her family and friends. The antiheroine is remote and self-centered; she lives for herself. The antiheroine stops at nothing to get what she wants, even if by achieving her goal she harms others. Women like Canfield's Eugenia Mills, Norris' Isabelle Carter, or Bailey's Adelaide Laramore often try to preserve their youthful features in order to attract their man—who is frequently already promised or married to the heroine. Adroit and cunning, the "Other Woman" frequently uses underhanded methods to attain her goal, tactics which the heroine would never dream of employing. Chief among these tactics, of course, is the antiheroine's exploitation of her sex appeal. Young villainesses are as likely to take such measures as are older ones. When Ella Bishop's young cousin Amy comes to live with her in Bess Streeter Aldrich's *Miss Bishop* (1933), the apparently guileless Amy wastes no time in appropriating Ella's fiancé Delbert—by spending the night with him on a river excursion while Ella is attending a faculty meeting. Similarly, in Ellen Glasgow's *Vein of Iron* (1935), when Ada Fincastle unwisely tells selfish, spoiled Janet Rowan of her secret engagement to Ralph McBride, Janet heartlessly proceeds to take Ralph away from Ada. Too late Ada reflects that her aunt had called Janet a "born troublemaker." (131)

Although the heroine suffers anguish when the antiheroine is successful at ensnaring her sweetheart, the heroine's pain is as nothing compared to what is in store for the unlucky male prey. As soon as the wedding is over, the siren becomes a shrew, making life hell for her new husband. In Bess Streeter Aldrich's *Spring Came on Forever* (1935), schoolteacher Myrtie Bates wins Joe Holmsdorfer's affections away from his longtime sweetheart Rose Schaffer. Once he has married Myrtie, Joe soon wishes he had been loyal to Rose. His new wife persuades Joe to provide her with luxuries which he cannot afford; she insists that Joe Americanize his name to Holms, thereby succeeding in compelling him publicly to reject his family traditions. Eventually, Myrtie talks her husband into giving up his beloved farm and mortgaging his land in order to buy a house in town, so that Myrtie can be closer to her friends. It is not until Joe loses his town house during the Depression that he finally realizes that he should never have acceded to Myrtie's demands.

Ellen Kimball, who marries the protagonist's brother John in Mary Ellen Chase's *Mary Peters* (1934), makes an equally unsatisfactory wife. Apparently pliant and gentle as a girl, Ellen turns out to be rigid and self-centered once she is married. Unlike Myrtie, who finds housekeeping tiresome, Ellen keeps her house in exemplary order. Nevertheless, John finds that Ellen's neatness has its price: "She ran the house with an iron hand, irritated at the slightest trace of disorder. . . . He grew slowly used to her complaints and impatient corrections [of the hired girl] and began to see the wisdom in staying away except when summoned at mealtimes." (252–53) Like Joe Holmsdorfer, John Peters had expected that his wife would take an interest in his farm, but John's expectations are no more realized than Joe's. Only too soon John comes to understand that his wife threatens his very way of life. Chase writes,

John Peters found himself steadily faced by an adversary of whose stealthy approach he had been for a full year uncomfortably aware. This adversary was his life with Ellen, and it was engaged in pushing him back to the wall where he must defend himself for the sake of the claim upon him of the other and larger life he knew [his partnership with nature as a farmer]. (261–62)

Unlike Joe Holmsdorfer, John Peters has recognized in time the threat that his wife represents. He hardens himself against Ellen's pleas and complaints, and Ellen finds to her dismay that John has "somehow grown as irrestible as the weather itself." (264)

Maxim de Winter, in Daphne du Maurier's *Rebecca* (1938), finds his wife more difficult to ignore. Like Joe Holmsdorfer and John Peters, Maxim de Winter soon discovers that he has been deluded as to his wife's true nature. Although Rebecca seemed "so lovely, so accomplished, so amusing" (272), in reality she was corrupt and vulgar. Unfaithful to her husband, she kept a flat in London for liaisons with her lovers. More than merely self-centered, Rebecca was fundamentally evil, promising Maxim that she would "look after your precious Manderley for you, make it the most famous show-place in the country, if you like. And people will . . . say we are the luckiest, happiest, handsomest couple in all England." (273) In return, Maxim must keep quiet about her frequent trips to London, about the love-trysts in the boathouse. Anxious to preserve his reputation, Maxim accepts Rebecca's conditions and the two maintain the facade of a happily married couple—until the day Rebecca announces her pregnancy to him and gloatingly predicts that one day her son will inherit Maxim's beloved Manderley. Maxim shoots her dead, unaware that Rebecca has goaded him to murder her, not because she is with child, but because she has an incurable disease. Rebecca is as evil a woman as they come in popular fiction of the interwar period—or in practically any other period, for that matter. A malevolent wife, she would have been as emotionally incapable of motherhood as she was physically unable to bear a child due to a "malformation of the uterus." (367)

Given Rebecca's personality, it was fortunate that she could not have children. In most popular women's novels of the period, antiheroines make poor mothers. From the start, they are dismayed to learn that they are pregnant. In Norris' *Rose of the World* (1924), Jack Talbot rejects heroine Rose Kirby to marry self-centered Edith Rogers. Edith is displeased when she finds she is pregnant. Disregarding her doctor's warnings, she continues riding her horse. One doubts that any Norris reader shed a tear when Edith has a fall, suffers a miscarriage, and dies. In Chase's *Mary Peters*, Ellen Kimble Peters is equally unhappy when she learns that she is with child. Once the baby is born, she regards it as a nuisance. Against her husband's and the doctor's advice, she overfeeds it and doses it with paregoric so that the baby will be quiet and not disturb her. Ellen's mistreatment of her child leads to its death. Bess Streeter Aldrich's Myrtie Holms, in *Spring Came on Forever* (1935), may not kill off her fetus or her baby, but she is scarcely a good mother to her son Neal. As Aldrich comments, "Myrtie's love for him took a queer expression for a mother. Apparently it consisted for the most part in wanting him to be talented and courteous and to show off before her friends." (211) Myrtie finds that caring for her son interferes with her social life. Claiming that her health is too delicate to permit her to raise the child, she often leaves little Neal with his grandmother. All in all, Myrtie displays little genuine feeling for her son. A typical antiheroine, she is too self-absorbed to care for anyone but herself.[2]

If villainesses like Rebecca de Winter, Ellen Peters, Edith Talbot, and Myrtie Holms are motivated by their self-interest to disregard the needs of their husbands and children, heroines disinterestedly seek to secure the happiness of their loved ones before their own. In some of the popular novels of the time, the heroines are eventually rewarded for their self-denial. In Kathleen Norris' *Rose of the World*, for instance, Rose refuses to divorce the villainous Clyde Bainbridge, fearing that, if she does so, he may try to gain custody of their daughter. For the sake of her little girl, therefore, Rose stoically endures Bainbridge's irrational anger toward her—until he is conveniently killed and Rose is free to marry her true love. Similarly, in Bailey's *The Dim Lantern*, Jane Barnes forces herself to accept the proposal of wealthy Frederick Towne, whom she does not love, in order to engage an expensive medical specialist to save her sister's life. In *The Dim Lantern*, as in *Rose of the World*, all works out well in the end. Jane's brother wins a magazine illustration contest and uses the prize money to repay Towne, thereby releasing Jane from her engagement. Jane can now marry the man she loves, and everyone except perhaps Towne lives happily ever after.

Most heroines of popular women's novels of the Twenties and Thirties are not rewarded quite so directly for their self-abnegating deeds. For some heroines, their decisions build their character rather than win them the man they love. In Margaret Ayer Barnes' *Years of Grace* (1930), Jane Carver's refusal to desert her family for Jimmy Trent helps to mold her into a stronger, more self-reliant person. As Jane watches her daughter submit to the temptation which she herself had withstood, she wonders if something is "missing in the moral fiber" of the members of her daughter's generation. "Did decency mean nothing to them? Did loyalty? Did love?" (534) Jane may have sacrificed high romance, but she can take satisfaction in the way that she has met her duty as a wife and mother.

A novel with somewhat the same theme as that of *Years of Grace* is *The Age of Innocence* (1920), which was one of the best-selling novels of 1921 and which enabled Edith Wharton to become the first woman to receive the Pulitzer Prize. In this book the author details Newland Archer's growing infatuation with his fiancée's cousin in late-nineteenth-century New York. Before he encounters the Countess Olenska, Archer is drawn to propose to May Welland because he is attracted by her maidenly innocence. After Ellen Olenska has arrived upon the scene, Archer begins to wonder if May's "niceness" were "only a negation, the curtain dropped before an emptiness." (171) His placid love for the unsophisticated May is replaced by a tempestuous passion for the more mature, worldly Ellen. Archer is ready to break his engagement to May, but Ellen stops him. She asserts that he has taught her a higher ethic: she cannot now accept "happiness bought by disloyalty and cruelty and indifference." (142) Despite a temporary weakening of their resolve, Ellen soon moves back to Europe to live alone, and Archer resigns himself to his marriage to May. The lovers have sacrificed their happiness to protect May. Wharton scholar Cynthia Griffin Wolff calls *The Age of Innocence* a "coming-of-age novel." By renouncing Ellen in order to remain with May, Newland Archer has "rejected notions of narcissistic self-fulfillment for the responsibility of 'establishing and guiding the next generation'; and in solving the problems of love, he has accepted the problems of care." (1977, 328) Wharton's Newland Archer, like Barnes' Jane Carver, has achieved a "grace" of character by placing duty above self-interest.[3]

For Newland Archer and Jane Carver, sacrifice is a single act, an act, moreover, which eventually recedes into memory, prompting only fleeting, blunted pain when recalled in later years. For O-lan in Pearl S. Buck's *The Good Earth* (1931), on the other hand, life is a continual series of sacrifices. Just over a decade after *The Age of Innocence* appeared, Buck, the daughter of American missionaries to China, published *The Good Earth*, her first major novel. One of the most popular works of fiction of the decade, the book ranked first on the best-seller lists for both 1931 and 1932, was translated into more than thirty languages, and earned its author the Pulitzer Prize for 1932. *The Good Earth* was dramatized for Broadway and later made into a successful movie in 1937, gaining actress Luise Rainer an Oscar for her performance. *The Good Earth*, like *The Age of Innocence*, features a male protagonist. Wang Lung is a poor Chinese farmer who becomes the richest man in his district before the end of the novel. A major secondary character is O-lan, the slave whom Wang Lung buys as his wife. O-lan serves her husband faithfully. She bears him sons, works beside him in the fields, and makes him a wealthy man when she finds a cache of jewels left behind by those fleeing the enemy during a civil war. Despite O-lan's quiet loyalty, Wang Lung comes to despise her for her peasant origins, and he transfers his attentions to a younger, prettier woman. Even though she is hurt by Wang Lung's rejection, O-lan continues to work for her husband's welfare as long as she still draws breath. Wang Lung owes his prosperity entirely to O-lan, but it is only upon her death that he admits his debt to her. When she is buried, Wang Lung thinks to himself, "There in that land of mine is buried the first good half of my life and more. It is as though half of me were buried there." (232) Because this story is told from Wang Lung's point of view, O-lan never comes into sharp focus as the heroine of this novel. We admire her unselfishness and we regret that Wang Lung does not appreciate her sacrifices for him, but we are not emotionally caught up in her life. Without access to her thoughts and given her taciturnity, we have only a vague notion as to what she is feeling at any given point in the book.

In *Lummox* (1923) Fannie Hurst presents a character who is equally as wordless as O-lan but, because Hurst allows us to be privy to her thoughts, we empathize with Bertha to a degree impossible with O-lan. While most fictional heroines make sacrifices for their families only, Bertha, a domestic servant who works for various employers in New York City, places the interests of all with whom she comes into contact above her own. As Margaret Lawrence remarks in *The School of Femininity* (1936), Fannie Hurst follows Bertha "on and on through her service to people, going here and going there, as if in response to the string of fate, never expecting either appreciation or reward, and not even any slight amount of understanding. It is a Messianic story—the beloved story of the Jews"—with Bertha as the Christ-figure. (195)

Hurst suggests that Bertha's ultimate sacrifice is that of giving up her son, whom she has borne out of wedlock, to the Bixbys, a wealthy Chicago couple who can raise the boy in the comfort which Bertha cannot provide. When the boy is five, Bertha learns that the Bixbys have resettled in New York City, and she moves in with their rather repulsive chauffeur Willy in order to have firsthand news of her son. For the boy's birthday, she persuades Willy to take the child her concertina, a shabby heirloom from the Old Country. Immediately drawn to his birthday gift, he plays it incessantly. Presumably it is from Bertha and his forebears that he has derived his love for music: Hurst tells us that one of Bertha's ancestors was a composer "whose melodies were to wind down through the centuries . . . and whose precious, groping old songs . . . were locked in the heart of Bertha" (171–72)—who passes them on to her son, who becomes a famous piano composer. Bertha herself attends one of his concerts, standing humbly in the back of the concert hall and deeply moved by the music, never realizing that she is listening to her own son performing one of his compositions.

This tableau in which a mother stands inconspicuously in the background, silent witness to her child's triumphant entry into a social world into which the parent cannot hope to be admitted, recalls to us the famous scene in Olive Higgins Prouty's *Stella Dallas*, also published in 1923, in which Stella unobtrusively watches from the alleyway beside a New York mansion as her daughter's wedding takes place inside. First filmed in 1925 and remade into the classic 1937 version by director King Vidor with Barbara Stanwyck and John Boles,[4] *Stellas Dallas*, like *Lummox*, features a heroine who is working-class—a relatively uncommon social status for the female protagonist of a best-selling women's novel of this period.

While Bertha has no desire to better her social class, the same is not true for Stella, who woos and wins the well-born Stephen Dallas. The disparity in their backgrounds quickly leads to trouble. Prouty presents Stephen as cultured and genteel, Stella as ignorant and vulgar. Stephen eventually leaves his wife—and their small daughter Laurel—and moves to New York to join a prestigious law firm. Regretting Stephen's absence only because it compromises her social position, Stella increasingly centers her attention upon Laurel. Stella had little interest in the child when it was a baby, but her maternal feelings do not take long to surface. Soon, Laurel has become the center of her life. She transfers her effort to rise above her station to the attempt to attain this goal for her daughter. If Stella herself cannot achieve social success, she is determined that Laurel will do so. Stella scrimps and saves on Stephen's monthly allowance to send Laurel to private school, to pay for riding and dancing lessons, and to purchase fashionable clothing for her. Despite Stella's pains, Laurel is not accepted by the daughters of the "better" families. The problem, although neither Laurel nor Stella realizes it, is Stella herself. She has successfully prepared Laurel to look and act the part of a refined lady, but Stella's appearance and behavior has become more and more flamboyantly inappropriate as she approaches middle age. As Prouty writes, "Mrs. Dallas was like certain dressmakers, who know how to impart elegance and refinement to the clothes they make for others, while their own costumes are often extreme and unpleasantly conspicuous." (14)

Although Stephen Dallas has no interest in seeing his wife, he encourages Laurel to visit him every summer. Genuinely fond of his daughter, he introduces her to art and music and good books, hoping to counteract Stella's influence in forming the child's taste. Since leaving Stella, Stephen has become reacquainted with Helen Morrison, his boyhood sweetheart who is now a widow with three sons. Helen is the very antithesis of Stella, at least in outward appearance and manner. Stephen muses, "Stella and Helen were as unlike as a wax figure, with highly colored cheeks, glass eyes, and blond hair, is unlike a statue of a beautiful Diana carved in white marble." (156) Stephen introduces Laurel to Helen, and his daughter immediately worships her—while loyally retaining first place in her heart for her mother.

The summer that Laurel is seventeen, it becomes painfully clear to both mother and daughter that Stella herself is standing in the way of Laurel's social advancement. They overhear one woman remark of Laurel that "[i]t's like having a ball and chain around her ankle to be obliged to drag a woman like that after her wherever she goes." (189) Stella decides to grant her husband a divorce so that he can marry Helen and then to send Laurel to live with them permanently. All goes according to Stella's plan—until Laurel is told of it. Laurel stubbornly declines to turn her back on her mother and refuses to leave her. Stella is forced to take more drastic action. She marries alcoholic and drug addicted Ed Munn, a coarse man whom Laurel detests. Disillusioned, Laurel returns to Stephen and Helen. While Stephen is inclined to believe that Stella's marriage proves that she is no good, Helen sees through Stella's scheme, murmuring "Greater love hath no woman than this." (231) Although Stella and Ed slide further and further into poverty as Ed spends more and more time in drug-induced unconsciousness, Stella has achieved what she has set out to do: Laurel has become "one of the most popular debutantes of the season." (240)

Stella has sacrificed everything for her child. By remarrying she has forfeited her monthly allowance from Stephen and, since Ed is in no shape to work, she is forced to take a job in a shirtwaist factory, an occupation she once would have disdained as beneath her. As her wages cover little more than the rent for a single room in a cheap boardinghouse, Stella has no money, the author tells us, for new clothing, movies, or even desserts. Harder to endure is the fact that Stella has had to give up Laurel's love and respect. As Stephen exclaims angrily, "To think she was willing to allow her child's wonderful love for her, her child's wonderful loyalty to her, to become shame and scorn! To think of it!" (232) What makes Stella Dallas so touching a character is, as film historian Molly Haskell observes, "not her self-pity but, on the contrary, her absolute refusal to feel sorry for herself. We supply what these heroines hold back. Who can help weeping all the tears refused by the laughing-on-the-outside bravura of . . . Barbara Stanwyck in *Stella Dallas*?" (1974, 184)

Yet, when we stop and think, we may begin to wonder whether Stella's goal is worth the heartache required to achieve it. The novel, like the films, is based upon the premise that it is morally and materially better to be upper-class than lower-class.[5] Stella's willingness to risk Laurel's love for the sake of her daughter's happiness may prove that Stella has a heart of gold despite her working-class exterior of base metal, but Stella seemingly cannot escape the inferiority of her lower-class origins. Even though Stella comes to accept the fact that she is "common" and is destined to remain so, she wants her daughter to have a "better" life, a concept which she associates with social advancement. Laurel herself seems less caught up with her mother's dream of social mobility. When she refuses at first to abandon her mother in order to live with her father and his new wife, Laurel proposes that she become a stenographer, an idea which Stella finds appalling: "Laurel wearing paper cuffs and elastic bands and pencils in her hair; eating lunch out of a box with a lot of other girls, also wearing paper cuffs and elastic bands and pencils in their hair? No. No. It mustn't be. It simply mustn't be. Why, even she herself wouldn't have been a stenographer." (218) The problem is not so much, as Haskell asserts, that mothers like Stella Dallas push their children to "want 'more' " and thereby succeed in "creating monsters who will reject them and be 'ashamed' of them." (1974, 171) More to the point, it is Stella who wants "more" for Laurel and comes to be ashamed of herself.

If Stella Dallas makes one grand gesture of self-sacrifice for the sake of her daughter, Ray Schmidt in Fannie Hurst's *Back Street* (1931) devotes her entire life to maintaining the happiness of her lover through her own self-denial. Made into a movie with John Boles and Irene Dunne in 1932, remade with Margaret Sullavan and Charles Boyer in 1941, and filmed with Susan Hayward and John Gavin in 1961, *Back Street* opens in Cincinnati in the 1890s. Ray Schmidt is eighteen, attractive, and stylish. A clerk and buyer in her father's dress trimming store, Ray goes out with all the traveling salesmen who come to town. Although sexually attracted to none of them, she nevertheless lets them kiss her. Ray just can't say no. "How easy it was to give pleasure. Your own pleasure was the result of giving that pleasure. To say 'no' hurt more than the dilemma of granting a reluctant 'Yes.' That had always been Ray's particular predicament." (16) It is not until Ray meets Walter Saxel, a young bank clerk who is engaged to the daughter of a prominent and highly respectable Cincinnati family, that Ray finally falls in love. Walter seems almost on the verge of breaking his engagement to

Corinne Trauer when family duties force Ray to stand Walter up on the morning he is to introduce her to his mother. Walter marries Corinne, and seven years pass before Ray and Walter meet again. By this time, Ray is working as a stock supervisor in a Manhattan dress fittings company; Walter is a junior partner in a Wall Street banking house. He soon asks Ray to allow him to install her in a small apartment of her own, where he can come and go when he likes. Once she is settled, Walter persuades her to quit her job so that she will be home whenever he needs to talk to her.

As the years go by, Walter and Ray's relationship settles into one characterized not so much by illicit romance as by domesticity. Walter drops by Ray's little apartment when he needs to relax, and Ray puts aside her own cares to devote herself to comforting him. She also helps him in more material ways. She has considerably more financial acumen than Walter, and she unobtrusively helps him decide on the wisest course to take in complex business transactions. Although Walter is nervous about being able to progress in the family banking house, Ray knows that "Walter would not fail. . . . He would succeed in the way the slow, the plodding, the bitterly tenacious, and the unbrilliant can succeed. Properly guided, always properly guided . . . he would succeed." (194)

Despite Ray's devotion to Walter, he persists in taking her for granted, "[t]o come to her for reassurance and coaxing. To think only of himself, and never of her." (367) Thus, Walter's attitude and behavior toward Ray is not so different from Wang Lung's toward O-lan in *The Good Earth*. Although Ray does not expect a return on her faithfulness to Walter, she cannot avoid seeing that Walter has amassed a fortune and that, although he spends liberally on his wife and children, he is almost miserly when it comes to Ray. She does not complain about being forced to live frugally, but she does begin to worry about her future. What will she do if Walter dies without leaving any financial provision for her? Walter does just that, and Ray's worst fears are realized. She slowly sinks into destitution, finally dying of starvation in a rented room in Aix-les-Bains.

Ray Schmidt's life is one of total sacrifice. She gives up her independence, her honor, her self-respect, her financial security, and her chance to have children to make Walter happy, and the worst thing is that he is too fatuous and self-centered to realize, much less appreciate, what she has renounced for him. While some readers may have admired Ray for her selfless devotion to the man she loves, others may well have wondered whether her unselfishness was worth the cost, given her lover's lack of character and his insensitivity toward her.[6] Fannie Hurst appears to have been more interested in probing the psychology of a character who is willing to give up everything for the man she loves rather than in trying to convince readers that the character's suffering is worthy of esteem. While readers of women's popular novels seem to have accepted the notion that heroines should be intrinsically self-sacrificing and, in this case, may have identified and empathized with Ray Schmidt's plight, usually the women's novels of the day demonstrated that self-renunciation was worth the pain and inconvenience it caused. The heroine herself may not have been rewarded directly, but she could take pride in the fact that, through her sacrifice, others—others whom the reader recognized as deserving of the heroine's efforts—gained happiness or achieved success. Book and movie audiences, for instance, may have been moved by the pathos of Stella Dallas standing in the rain outside the window on her daughter's wedding day; at the same time, however, they could also acknowledge that Stella herself is triumphant at witnessing her daughter's entry into the world of the social elite, and they could be satisfied that Laurel was worth the sacrifice. Laurel would not have hesitated to forfeit her own happiness for the sake of her mother, had their roles been reversed. On the other hand, a heroine like Ray Schmidt, whose selflessness is lavished upon a character who seems undeserving of it, seems tragic—or duped by an ideology which has failed her.[7]

Less problematic in its portrayal of unselfishness rewarded is a novel we have discussed earlier in this chapter, Daphne du Maurier's *Rebecca*, the vehicle for yet another highly successful film. Produced by David O. Selznick, directed by Alfred Hitchcock, and starring Laurence Olivier and Joan Fontaine, the movie was released in 1940. Rebecca and the second Mrs. de Winter are almost textbook examples of the "Bad Woman" and the "Good Woman." As Carol Thurston remarks, Rebecca is

sophisticated, self-confident, and beautiful, all the things the plain, naive, awkward, and thoroughly inadequate second Mrs. de Winter is not. . . . In the end, it turns out that Max loves her for the very attributes she was so sure made her unlovable: her physical plainness, unassuming goodness, loyalty, her dependency on him, and, of course, her sexual näiveté. (1987, 41)

If Rebecca is Donald Makosky's "vampire temptress," who uses her sexuality to achieve power, her successor is her opposite: she is sexually inexperienced and regards physical passion as appropriate only as an expression of emotional intimacy. Rebecca is fundamentally and irredeemably self-centered; her successor seeks only, at first, to please her husband Max and, later, to protect and comfort him. Despite the "Gothic" overtones of the plot and setting and the heroine's suffering throughout much of the book and movie, *Rebecca* ultimately has a happy ending. The heroine's selfless devotion to her husband pays off: Manderley may have burned to the ground, but the heroine has won Max's trust and love for life.[8] *Rebecca*, then, conforms to the conventions governing the characterization of heroine and anti-heroine in popular women's novels of the Twenties and Thirties. Unselfish and loyal, the heroine puts the welfare and interests of her husband before her own; the antiheroine is self-centered, unable or unwilling to contain her sexuality within conventional bounds, reluctant to assume maternal responsibilities. In *Rebecca*, the heroine's sacrifices are rewarded, in this case, directly: it is she, and not the antiheroine, who gains the affections of the hero.

Given the widespread use of opposing sets of character traits to distinguish heroine from antiheroine and given the fact that readers had come to expect that the protagonist would either win her man through her unselfishness or, in an apparently equally satisfying conclusion, would tragically sacrifice her happiness for the sake of the one she loved, it must have come as something of a shock when readers encountered the characters and plot of Margaret Mitchell's *Gone with the Wind* in 1936.

Among the popular novels of the day, *Gone with the Wind* can perhaps be more properly described as a blockbuster than as a best seller. As Darden Asbury Pyron remarks in his biography of Mitchell:

The publishing world had never experienced anything like this . . . by January 1937, sales had topped one million copies in the United States alone. They rose inexorably through the new year. In the spring of 1937, the American Booksellers Association awarded *Gone with the Wind* its annual prize for the best fiction of the preceding year, and on May 4, the Pulitzer Committee announced Mitchell's capture of that crown, too. On the anniversary of publication, total sales swelled beyond 1,700,000. . . . Even in 1938, the printers still labored to supply the demand of booksellers for over 1,000 copies every month. And by now, too, foreign presses were milling out their translations by the thousands and the tens of thousands. (1991, 336)[9]

The movie rights to the book were sold to the man who would soon produce the film version of *Rebecca*, David O. Selznick, who paid $50,000, a price which set a new record in the industry. (Pyron 1991, 355) Amid great fanfare, Selznick set about casting the film, eventually settling upon Vivien Leigh, an English actress relatively unknown in the United States, to play Scarlett O'Hara and Clark Gable to play Rhett Butler. The movie was as wildly successful as the book. In her study of reader response to both book and movie, Helen Taylor notes that, since the film's opening in Atlanta on December 15, 1939, it

has been seen by more people than the entire population of the USA. . . . It has been subtitled in twenty-four languages, dubbed into six. Of thirteen nominations, it was awarded eight Oscars, including the first ever to a black actor, Hattie McDaniel. It is regularly referred to as the greatest film ever made. (1989, 2)

Given the enormous popularity of *Gone with the Wind*, it is perhaps surprising that its heroine bears little resemblance to the other fictional heroines of the day. Mitchell later wrote that she "set out to depict a far-from-admirable woman about whom little that was good could be said." (Quoted in Wood 1983, 135) and her characterization of Scarlett O'Hara demonstrates that she achieved her goal. There is no question that in many respects Scarlett is truly a ruthless, offensive human being. She is nasty to her children, who are afraid of her; she steals two women's fiancés, one of the women being her own sister, and she continually tries to take Ashley away from his wife; she insists on returning to Tara the night that her sister-in-law Melanie gives birth—at considerable risk to the health of mother and child; she is responsible for the "mindless sacrifice of her [second] husband's life" (Fox-Genovese 1981, 400); upon her third marriage, she tastelessly flaunts her wealth; she allows her foreman to mistreat her convict laborers, even though she is well aware that his methods are likely to lead to their death. As Elizabeth Fox-Genovese notes, "Mitchell makes scant effort to redeem Scarlett from the stark self-interest and greed of her chronicled behavior. On the contrary, from the opening pages of the novel . . . she establishes the fundamental contours of Scarlett's grasping personality." (400–401) Fox-Genovese suggests that, because "Scarlett never attained that psychological identification with her mother which would have provided the bedrock for her becoming her mother's successor" (404), Scarlett is unable to achieve "acceptance of herself as a woman." (402) Perhaps more serious is the charge that Scarlett is unable to internalize an adult moral code which would allow her to operate as a mature human being with a fully-developed superego.[10]

It is Scarlett's sister-in-law Melanie Wilkes and not Scarlett herself who is presented from the first as having the characteristics of the typical heroine. As Rhett Butler tells Scarlett, "If I am "nicer" to Mrs. Wilkes, it is because she deserves it. She is one of the very few kind, sincere, and unselfish persons I have ever known." (Mitchell 1936, 223) Scarlett herself tends to sell Melanie short, mistaking Melanie's gentleness for weakness and hating Melanie for unwittingly preventing Scarlett from marrying Ashley Wilkes. It is not until Melanie is dying that Scarlett finally realizes how much she has depended on her, "that Melanie has always been there beside her with a sword in her hand, unobtrusive as her own shadow, loving her, fighting for her with blind passionate loyalty, fighting Yankees, fire, hunger, poverty, public opinion and even her beloved blood kin." (1012)[11]

In attempting to analyze Scarlett O'Hara as a literary character, one must confront the fact that Margaret Mitchell as author is much less directive than most popular novelists in indicating what we are to make of her famous protagonist. And, as Southern Renaissance scholar Richard King observes,

if there was confusion in literary characterization, Mitchell was no clearer in her private correspondence or her public statements about Scarlett. In a letter of July 1936 she claimed that Scarlett was a "normal person," but she countered later by writing a friend that "Scarlett was not a very nice person." Then, early in 1937, Mitchell came down squarely on both sides by allowing that Scarlett "had good traits . . . balanced by her bad qualities." (1983, 180)

Although in one of her letters she claimed that "Melanie Wilkes and the matrons of Atlanta were the true heroines in the novel" (Quoted by O'Brien 1983, 165), at the premiere of the film in Atlanta she "repeatedly thanked her audience and the filmmakers for what they had done for her and 'my Scarlett.' " (King 1983, 180)

For contemporary critics of the novel, the ambiguity of Scarlett's characterization made it difficult for them to pigeonhole the heroine. A *New York Times* book reviewer observed in some confusion that Scarlett O'Hara was a "heroine lacking in many virtues—in nearly all, one might say, but courage. She is a vital creature, this Scarlett, alive in every inch of her, selfish, unprincipled, ruthless, greedy and dominating, but with a backbone of supple, springing steel." (J. Donald Adams, quoted in Dwyer 1983, 23) The reviewer for the *Churchman* was equally divided in his praise and censure, remarking that "Scarlett is not an admirable character, utterly selfish, yet capable of heroism in her indomitable efforts to preserve the old estate." (*Churchman*, Sept. 1, 1936, 18) While the *Boston Transcript* proclaimed Scarlett a "heroine to be long remembered" (*Boston Transcript*, June 27, 1936, 1), the *New Republic* questioned the morality of a protagonist who "wants only to last and takes any terms life offers." (*New Republic*, July 15, 1936, 301) As Richard King remarks, the novel "offers something for everyone. Ambiguous without being complex, it allows those nostalgic for a lost way of life their innings yet apotheosizes its very negation, the woman on the make. But then it turns around and gives the raven-haired hussy her comeuppance—and ends with her indomitably setting forth again." (1983, 181)

In *Scarlett's Women: Gone with the Wind and Its Female Fans* (1989), Helen Taylor suggests that, although reader response to Scarlett O'Hara has always been mixed, it is still possible to discern a basic pattern in the terms by which readers, critics, and scholars have judged her. During the Depression and War years, Scarlett was most frequently praised for her ability to survive in a hostile world. As times changed, Taylor finds that the "allowances which women of a previous generation made for Scarlett's selfishness and single-mindedness because 'she worked and schemed the whole time to keep Tara not just for herself but for her family' are unnecessary for later generations, who tend to see Scarlett as an example of gutsy individualism or feminist self-determination." (101) Scarlett the survivor is replaced in many readers' minds by Scarlett the rebellious modern woman.[12]

Anne Goodwyn Jones and Elizabeth Fox-Genovese are two scholars who argue that Margaret Mitchell is attempting to come to terms with changing expectations of female behavior in her characterization of Scarlett O'Hara. They have observed that Mitchell—who was born in 1900, began writing her novel in 1926, and virtually completed it three years later—was herself a product of the Twenties, an era in which women were beginning to reexamine traditional gender roles. Fox-Genovese argues that

"Mitchell's ambivalent attitudes towards female sexuality, gender identity, and gender role—desire, womanhood, and ladyhood—informed her own life, as well as the life of her heroine." (1981, 407) According to Jones, Mitchell's ambivalence lay in the fact that her mother and "the other women of her own and earlier generations" bequeathed to Mitchell the belief that women should be self-sacrificing and ladylike but, at the same time, provided in their own actions the contradictory evidence that Southern women could be competent, powerful, and tough. (Jones 1981, 328) While an older generation of women writers could continue to create characters embodying both of these sets of traits without apparently recognizing any conflict between them, as we have seen most clearly in the treatment of farm and pioneer heroines in Bess Streeter Aldrich's *A Lantern in Her Hand* and *Spring Came On Forever*, Edna Ferber's *So Big*, and Gladys Hasty Carroll's *As the Earth Turns*, the younger Mitchell found it more difficult to fashion a heroine who combined these sets of characteristics. "By the time Mitchell came of age," Jones writes,

these two strands of womanhood—velvet and steel—had separated within her immediate culture into, on the one hand, the admonition of traditionalists that women be dependent, sacrificial, pious, pure, and self-deprecatory; and on the other, into the Jazz Age "freedom" that loosened the straitjacket of "hard-boiled" women's sexuality and language. (1981, 328)

Unlike the traditional heroine, Scarlett is not passive, self-effacing, domestic, dependent, submissive, and passionless. While her refusal to adopt these traits causes her to forfeit her chance to be regarded by her fellow characters as a "lady" and elicited some consternation among those readers who had come to expect their heroines to uphold the very standards which Scarlett defies, Melanie's presence in the novel served to provide such readers with a more satisfyingly conventional heroine. Furthermore, readers could view Rhett's desertion of Scarlett at the end of the novel as just retribution for Scarlett's failings as a heroine. In assessing her respondents' reactions to the ending, Helen Taylor speculates that the conclusion perhaps "satisfies our sense of rough justice and our desire as reader-viewers to see Scarlett punished for that major crime in fictional texts, her lack of self-knowledge and misrecognition of love" (1989, 153)—and, we might add, her self-absorption and selfishness.

Despite the fact that women found it hard to condone all of her actions, Scarlett O'Hara has won the hearts of readers for generation after generation more effectively than any conventional romantic heroine. Perhaps, as Taylor's study suggests, Scarlett's continuing popularity signals the emergence of a new generation of women readers, with a different set of experiences and values from those which prevailed among readers of the Twenties and Thirties. Perhaps her acceptance in the postwar years marks the beginning of a widespread dissatisfaction among middle-class women with their roles and status. And yet . . . we must keep in mind that the most popular heroines in the second half of the twentieth century have been the protagonists of the Harlequin Romances and their imitators. These fictional women, at least until recently, have been sexually inexperienced, passive, dependent—and delighted at the prospect of marrying the "right" man at the novel's end. This is hardly the characterization or the plot employed by Margaret Mitchell in *Gone with the Wind*.

On the other hand, the paperback romance formula is not so different from the conventions used in other popular women's novels of the Twenties and Thirties. Just as feminist critics have noted the conservative cast given to gender relationships in postwar Harlequin Romances, so we can discern a similar treatment in popular women's novels of the interwar period. By extolling their heroines' self-sacrificing behavior, best-selling women writers reflect traditional notions of female social roles: women are expected to devote themselves to furthering the interests and happiness of their husbands and children at the expense of their own needs and wishes. Such a conception of womanly responsibility countered the image of the "New Woman" gaining currency in the Twenties. Rather than focusing upon their own self-actualization, upon their own demands and desires, women were to follow in their mothers' and grandmothers' footsteps and submerge their needs in order to satisfy those of their families. More progressive in her approach to gender issues, Dorothy Canfield used another tack in handling her heroine's decision to remain with her husband and children in *The Brimming Cup*. As we have seen in an earlier chapter, Canfield refuses to treat as a moral issue Marise Crittenden's temptation to accept Vincent Marsh's entreaties that she leave town with him. Instead, Canfield gives the reader to understand that this crisis is an opportunity for Marise to gain self-confidence, to articulate for herself her own values, and to make the choice which seems right for her. While Marise, like the protagonists of other novels of the period, eventually decides to stay with Neale and her children, Canfield, like Glasgow in *Barren Ground*, stands out from the other Twenties novelists we have discussed in that she suggests that female self-sacrifice is not automatically a virtue. More important for her characters, male and female alike, is self-reliance.

If the notion of womanly self-sacrifice could be used to combat the concept of the "New Woman" in the Twenties, the ideology of female sacrifice and martyrdom was equally relevant in the Thirties. As we have seen, the dramatic change in economic climate intensified public pressure upon women to stay at home and out of the paid labor force, where they were presumed to be competing with male breadwinners for scarce jobs. As the domestic ideology reasserted its hold upon the minds of many Americans, the notion of womanly sacrifice which had always been a central tenet in traditional assumptions regarding female behavior likewise gained strength. Only in *Gone with the Wind*, where the ability to survive appears to require more aggressive, even self-centered, traits, is a different set of female norms presented.

The postwar economic environment created the need, yet again, to foster a cultural climate in which women would place domestic responsibilities above all other concerns—and, in this case, to give up the jobs that they had gained during the War to male ex-servicemen. Films, best-selling novels, and popular magazine articles reemphasized women's roles as wives and mothers. The sacrificing heroine retained her place in American popular culture beyond the Twenties and Thirties into yet another era of American social history.

Conclusion

The novels discussed in this book were read by tens of thousands of women in the Twenties and Thirties. Few of them, however, are read, or even remembered, today. We recognize the titles, at least, of a handful of novels which were made into successful films, starring actors and actresses now regarded as stars. The movie versions of *The Sheik, Gone with the Wind, Rebecca,* "*Gentlemen Prefer Blondes,*" and *Stella Dallas* are broadcast on television, available on video, and even shown occasionally in movie houses. Yet, other best sellers which were captured on film and which featured well-known performers have faded from public memory. While some might faintly recall Bette Davis in the 1940 production of Rachel Field's *All This, and Heaven Too,* Laurence Olivier's starring role in the 1932 film version of Margaret Ayer Barnes' *Westward Passage* has long since been forgotten.

If Hollywood cannot guarantee a novel's lasting recognition, perhaps the growing attention given by feminist critics to particular books—and their movies—helps to revive or extend interest in specific works. During the past decade or two, scholars have published a number of articles analyzing such films as "*Gentlemen Prefer Blondes,*" *Stella Dallas, Rebecca,* and *Imitation of Life.* In some cases, critics have argued that the heroines in these films are subverting patriarchal expectations of women; in other instances, writers have contended that the female leads are trapped in inflexible and restrictive gender roles. While such analyses contribute to our understanding of these fictional characters, one doubts that such articles—appearing in professional journals like *Cinema Journal, Heresies,* and *Enclitic*—have had much effect upon the average middle-class woman's regard for the movies discussed— or for the novels upon which the movies are based.

One factor in retaining or increasing the popularity of older novels is availability. Most of the best sellers upon which this book has focused were removed long ago from the open shelves in public libraries. While some local libraries have discarded such novels altogether, others have stock-piled them in storage areas. As so-called "stack fiction," these books must be retrieved by special request; they cannot be rediscovered through brows-ing. If one looks at the fiction section of well-stocked bookstores, one does discover a handful of the titles examined in this book. Various feminist presses have reprinted older works by women. Virago, for instance, reis-sued Dorothy Canfield's *Her Son's Wife* in 1986. The Feminist Press repub-lished Josephine Johnson's *Now in November* in 1991. University presses have revived works by native daughters. The University of Indiana repub-lished Gene Stratton-Porter's *The Girl of the Limberlost* in 1984, and two years later the University of Nebraska Press brought out Bess Streeter Aldrich's *Miss Bishop*, one of four Aldrich books now available from Nebraska Press. Some of the big commercial publishing companies have also begun to reissue women's novels from the first half of the century. Signet-Vista, for instance, published Aldrich's *A Lantern in Her Hand* in 1983, and Signet Classics brought out Stratton-Porter's *A Girl of the Limberlost* in 1988, four years after Indiana Press had reintroduced the book. The majority of titles are published, however, not by feminist presses, academic publishing houses, or commercial conglomerates, but by small publishers who con-centrate on reprinting older books. Buccaneer Books has reissued E. M. Hull's *The Sheik* and *Son of the Sheik* and Caroline Miller's *Lamb in His Bosom*, as well as books by Temple Bailey and Gene Stratton-Porter. River City Press has reprinted some of Kathleen Norris' novels and yet more Stratton-Porter books. Cherokee Publishing, Greenwood Press, Amereon House, American Reprint Company, Peachtree Publishers, and Reprint Service have all reissued one or more novels by popular female—and male—writ-ers of the Twenties and Thirties.

While the reprinting of popular novels of the past by Buccaneer Books, River City Press, and the like is largely an effort to capitalize on older readers' nostalgia for the books of their youth,[1] the recent scramble by feminist, university, and mainstream commercial presses to republish the works of Dorothy Canfield, Josephine Johnson, Bess Streeter Aldrich, and other popular women novelists is a response to the increased focus on women's issues in colleges and universities. Even if feminist film and literary critics do not have a wide popular audience, they are influential among college English teachers, who have begun to include more women's titles on their booklists and thus to popularize women writers among college students. Following the awakening of interest in women's cultural heritage in the late 1960s and early 1970s, literature courses initially tended to focus upon the best-known "serious" women writers: Edith Wharton, Ellen Glasgow, and Willa Cather—and the works of these authors were the first to be reprinted. By the 1980s, attention had widened to include a number of lesser-known and more "popular" authors—hence the republication of the novels of Aldrich, Canfield, and Stratton-Porter. Women's studies programs have become increasingly common on campuses across the country over the past quarter-century, and reprint editions of women's novels are assigned in courses in this area as well as in courses offered under the aegis of English departments.

The recent efforts of book publishers to capitalize upon interest in some long-loved best sellers—and to renew interest in others which have been equally long forgotten—has had, thus far, only limited impact upon contemporary reception of these novels. While publishers have reprinted best sellers of the past, filmmakers have continued to produce movie versions of older popular novels. The 1990 remake of the classic 1937 film version of *Stella Dallas*, however, probably did little to renew enthusiasm for the 1923 novel, as *Stella* did poorly at the box office. Perhaps, Janet Maslin speculates in her *New York Times* review of the movie, audiences no longer accept the premise that class is the barrier to social advancement that it was deemed to be in 1937, when the Stanwyck movie was made, or in the Twenties, when the book first appeared. (1990, 18) Martin Scorsese's 1993 film *The Age of Innocence* starring Daniel Day-Lewis and Michelle Pfeiffer drew more critical acclaim—and larger audiences. As Wharton's *The Age of Innocence* is the only best seller written by a woman and published in the interwar era to have been accorded a secure position in the "canon" of recognized literary "classics," one suspects that the reputation of the novel and its author enhanced the reception of the movie—and not vice versa. The release of the Scorsese film indeed stimulated a modest increase in book sales, but the novel has been a steady seller for years.

While *The Age of Innocence* has long been regularly assigned in college literature courses, Pearl S. Buck's *The Good Earth* has been included in high-school English courses and on suggested reading lists. Many have read *The Age of Innocence* or *The Good Earth* because they have been directed to do so; more continue to read *Gone with the Wind* and *Rebecca* because they have chosen to read them. Never deemed by experts to be "superior" or "worthy" literature, these two books have, nevertheless, made the "strange and risky transformation from best-seller to cult to legend." (Beauman 1993, 127) Undoubtedly, these two books are among the most widely-read of the popular women's novels of the interwar era.

Perhaps nothing indicates more dramatically the continued popular interest in *Gone with the Wind* than the fact that Warner Books paid a $5.5 million advance to Alexandra Ripley, a South Carolina historical romance novelist, to write a sequel to the 1936 novel—or the fact that Warner then sold the television rights to Ripley's book to CBS for eight million dollars. Likewise, as a result of a "seven-figure publishing deal" (Beauman 1993, 128), Morrow brought out *Mrs. de Winter*, English novelist Susan Hill's sequel to Daphne du Maurier's *Rebecca*. Both sequels have sold well, and the media hype surrounding their publication has in turn stimulated sales of Mitchell's and du Maurier's original novels. Critics have generally found *Scarlett* and *Mrs. de Winter* inferior to their predecessors, but it is not clear that readers agree. During the first week *Scarlett* was on sale, for example, Warner Books estimated that five hundred thousand copies were sold nationwide. *Publishers' Weekly* reported that the "many negative reviews of the book seemed to have little effect on sales," according to booksellers throughout the country. One bookstore owner remarked, "I tell them, 'You don't want to buy it,' and they buy it anyway." (October 18, 1991, 12)

The publication of their sequels generated increased interest in the original novels, but neither had been in any danger of being forgotten. And, one suspects, women will continue to read *Gone with the Wind* (1936) and *Rebecca* (1938) long after *Scarlett* and *Mrs. de Winter* have lost their appeal. What is it about *Gone with the Wind* and *Rebecca* that has made these two books so popular? Perhaps the remoteness of their settings is one factor in their continued appeal: one takes place during the Civil War, while the action in the other occurs primarily in an isolated mansion in England. Thus, the novels can never seem dated in the way that books set in a contemporary middle-class milieu can. Also, as mentioned earlier, both were made into extremely successful movies which effectively captured the tone of the novels themselves. The continual re-release of the films in movie theaters and their availability on video have helped to keep the novels fresh in the public memory. Furthermore, both books are, on one level, love stories, a genre which has been popular with women readers at least since the publication of the Brontë sisters' novels in the mid-nineteenth century. Both novels were the progenitors of new types of romance fiction. The lengthy *Gone with the Wind* set the stage for the appearance of the career woman saga which Judith Krantz perfected in the 1980s, while *Rebecca*, which was itself a retelling of *Jane Eyre*, generated scores of imitations: so-called "Gothic" romances, set in faraway castles or mansions, combine romance with mystery in the plots of these books.

One suspects that, no matter how many other women's best sellers from the Twenties and Thirties are reprinted, added to college reading lists, analyzed by scholars, or translated into successful contemporary films, few books are likely to regain the readership they enjoyed in the past. As remarked upon earlier, best sellers tend to be "time-bound" (Lofroth, 15), to reflect the values and concerns of the era in which they are written. In the period in which these books were published, men and women had come to believe that marriage should be more than a relationship defined in terms of duties and sacrifice; they were beginning to expect matrimony to lead to emotional intimacy and companionship. At the same time, however, they still assumed that men and women should occupy separate marital spheres; they thought that the husband should take primary responsibility for providing the family's financial support while the wife should care for the children and keep house. In their novels, writers as different in theme and approach as Temple Bailey and Margaret Ayer Barnes articulate these marital expectations. While it was considered acceptable by the Twenties and Thirties for middle-class single women to enter the workplace, women were expected to quit their jobs upon marriage, as does Margaret Ross in Gladys Hasty Carroll's *As the Earth Turns* (1933). Between 1890 and 1990, the divorce rate in the United States would multiply tenfold. In the 1920s and 1930s, the rise in the divorce rate was remarked upon by magazine commentators—and by novelists. While popular women writers occasionally sided with characters who chose divorce, these writers were more likely to present such protagonists as wrongheaded, to suggest, as does Kathleen Norris, that few circumstances justified so drastic a step.

Underlying most fictional characterizations of women in the Twenties and Thirties is the notion that females are by nature unselfish. Setting aside their own needs and desires to satisfy those of their loved ones, they are the primary nurturers of their children, they hold their marriages together regardless of personal cost to themselves, and they do not complain when they must leave paying jobs to devote themselves full-time to their family. Self-abnegating they may be, but they are not weak. As the heroines of the farm and pioneer novels demonstrate most clearly, women characters may defer to their husbands and make sacrifices for their children, but they are also able to cope with crises and to shoulder responsibility for the farm should their male "providers" die, as does Selina DeJong's husband in Edna Ferber's *So Big* (1924). The female protagonists of non-farm novels are equally capable and strong, if less independent—as their husbands or fathers seldom suffer the early deaths which are often the lot of rural male characters. Ray Schmidt in Fannie Hurst's *Back Street* (1931), for instance, subtly guides her lover to business success and unfailingly provides him with emotional support—at the expense of her own happiness and financial security.

Over half a century after these books were written, women's expectations and values have changed. Premarital sex is no longer presumed to ruin a woman's reputation nor does the mere suspicion of sexual "wrongdoing" lead to a woman's social ostracism, as is the case in Norris' *The Foolish Virgin* (1929). Couples no longer feel obliged to marry after a single sexual encounter, as do Dot Haley and Eddie Collins in Vina Delmar's *Bad Girl* (1928). Male and female marital roles are not as rigidly defined by society as Dorothy Canfield shows them to be in *The Home-Maker* (1924). Men and women today share childrearing responsibilities while each pursues a career, and few regard such arrangements as unnatural or even unusual. While most view divorce as unfortunate—for the pain it occasions the separating spouses and for the turmoil it causes their children—few believe that divorce is invariably the woman's fault for not trying hard enough to keep the marriage from failing. And few believe that a marriage should be preserved at any cost.

Do women of today share none of the values middle-class women held in the Twenties and Thirties? Are contemporary women unable to relate to the experiences and perspectives of women of the interwar era? The fact that most best sellers of these past decades are now forgotten and are unlikely to achieve again the popularity they once enjoyed does not necessarily mean that they deal entirely with dead issues. Women are still socialized to place great emphasis upon marriage and family. While Gene Stratton-Porter, Kathleen Norris, and Temple Bailey novels have gone out of fashion, the romance genre which they helped to define is still the best-selling type of women's fiction. Although gender expectations have changed somewhat, girls are still brought up to be more concerned with building and maintaining relationships than with achieving success, as the latter goal is still widely thought to be more appropriate for men than for women. Females are expected to look after husbands, children, and aging parents—and to find satisfaction in their roles as caregivers. While many women—and men—have begun to rebel against these gender distinctions, women have found that, when they attempt to redefine their roles, to try, for example, to give equal time to family and career, they experience guilt for not fully playing the parts that they have been socialized to assume. Given the continuing, if increasingly conflicted, internalization of traditional gender expectations, heroines who sacrifice their own happiness for the sake of others still appeal to today's readers and movie audiences. We may disparage Stella's "knee-jerk nobility" and claim that Bette Midler's *Stella* enables us to "enjoy a good cry . . . for no good reason" (Maslin 1990, 18), but the fact remains that Stella's sacrifice *does* make us cry. On some basic level, we continue to be moved by a mother's selfless gesture.

Will the novels of the Twenties and Thirties enjoy a renaissance in the years ahead? Probably not. Even *Rebecca* and *Gone with the Wind* may appeal to fewer and fewer readers as gender expectations and social values undergo further change. *Rebecca* may have captured the interest of several succeeding generations of women readers, but, as the fashion in romance heroines turns toward feisty, independent, resourceful female protagonists, one doubts that contemporary readers will countenance much longer a heroine like the colorless, passive second Mrs. de Winter. Scarlett O'Hara possesses precisely those attributes which *Rebecca*'s protagonist lacks—and these are exactly the traits which characterize the heroines of Judith Krantz's best-selling novels. In *Princess Daisy* (1980), for example, one critic wrote that the women characters "take bold risks, court success unashamedly, and exhibit courage, toughness and fierce determination against overwhelming odds" (Gittelson 1980, 31)—just like Scarlett O'Hara. While Mitchell prolonged the life of her novel by providing readers with both an

"old-fashioned" heroine who conformed to gender expectations established in the nineteenth century and a "modern" heroine who is still
admired by late-twentieth-century readers—and imitated by popular writers—*Gone with the Wind* will eventually, one predicts, engage a dwindling
audience. Even if Mitchell's portrayal of women has worn well, her treatment of race may in time prompt readers to abandon the book. While her
attitude toward African-Americans indeed reflects the racial prejudice of
her era, it is a posture which is becoming less and less acceptable in an age
which prides itself on its commitment to "multi-culturalism"—in theory, if
not in practice. While the popular women's novels of the Twenties and
Thirties continue to address some concerns of importance to women of
today, they also deal with issues which have long been resolved. Contemporary women readers who happen upon popular women's novels of the
interwar era may find something of themselves and their concerns in the
heroines and their problems, but the fictional characters with whom the
present generation of readers is likely to relate most fully are the protagonists featured in women's novels published today.

Notes

INTRODUCTION

1. Obviously, we can do no more than speculate as to how readers responded to popular novels of the Twenties and Thirties. Furthermore, this study cannot prove that the attitudes presented in women's novels were held by a substantial proportion of their readers. The best way to provide conclusive evidence of readers' reactions to these books and of the relationship between readers' and novelists' values and assumptions is to interview readers, such as Janice Radway does when she questions a small number of romance novel readers in *Reading the Romance* (1984). Failing direct contact, the eliciting of letters and written questionnaires can also provide valuable insight regarding contemporary reader response, as Helen Taylor's *Scarlett's Women* (1989) makes clear. Since those women still alive today who read the best sellers of the Twenties and Thirties when the books were first published are now over half a century removed from their reading experience, it would be difficult for them to recall their initial responses to these books with any degree of reliability. For this reason, I felt that it would not be practical to attempt to reconstruct readers' responses and reactions to the novels examined herein. The one remaining approach would be to analyze letters written by readers to the various popular women novelists. Such an approach awaits a further study.

2. See Helen Waite Papashvily, *All the Happy Endings* (New York: Harper, 1956); and Nina Baym, *Women's Fiction: A Guide to Novels by and about Women in America, 1820–1870* (Ithaca, NY: Cornell, 1978). See also Jane Tompkins, *Sensational Designs: The Cultural Work of American Fiction, 1790–1860* (New York: Oxford, 1985); and Mary Kelley, *Private Woman, Public Stage: Literary Domesticity in Nineteenth-Century America* (New York: Oxford, 1984).

3. Feminist studies of contemporary mass-market romance include Jan Cohn, *Romance and the Erotics of Property: Mass-Market Fiction for Women* (Durham, North

Carolina: Duke University Press, 1988); Tania Modelski, "The Disappearing Act: A Study of Harlequin Romances," *Signs* 5 (1980): 434–48; Carol Thurston, *The Romance Revolution: Erotic Novels for Women and the Quest for a New Sexual Identity* (Urbana: University of Illinois Press, 1987); Leslie W. Rabine, "Romance in the Age of Electronics: Harlequin Enterprises," *Feminist Studies* 11 (Spring 1985): 39–60; Janice A. Radway, *Reading the Romance: Women, Patriarchy and Popular Literature* (Chapel Hill: University of North Carolina Press, 1984); and Ann Barr Snitow, "Mass Market Romance: Pornography for Women Is Different," *Radical History Review* 20 (Spring-Summer 1979): 141–61.

4. The two exceptions are E. M. Hull, who wrote *The Sheik* (1921), and Daphne du Maurier, who was the author of *Rebecca* (1938). Although both writers were English, their novels were hugely successful in this country: both books were among the top-ten best-selling novels in the American market for two years running. Futhermore, both books were made into Hollywood movies—*Rebecca* was Alfred Hitchcock's first American film—which were themselves warmly received by U.S. audiences. Given the spectacular popularity in America of these two books and the movies based upon them, they have been included in this study.

5. Olive Higgins Prouty's *Stella Dallas* (1923) never appeared on any monthly best-seller lists in the Twenties, let alone a yearly list. However, the success of the 1925 movie version of the book, the popularity of the 1937 remake directed by King Vidor and starring Barbara Stanwyck, and the warm reception of the long-running radio soap opera based upon the novel ensured the book a large and continued readership over a span of several decades.

Like *Stella Dallas*, Ursula Parrott's *Ex-Wife* (1929) was neither a monthly nor a yearly best seller. Unlike *Stella Dallas*, *Ex-Wife* was never made into a Hollywood movie, nor did it inspire a radio program. Nevertheless, *Ex-Wife* was scarcely ignored by the reading public, as the novel sold 100,000 copies. (Prose 1989, xi) *Ex-Wife* is introduced in this study to demonstrate that there was an alternative view to the issue of sexuality besides the one usually articulated by best-selling novelists, not to argue that Parrott is typical of popular women novelists with regard to her handling of this issue.

The third writer included in this study whose books were never listed on the monthly or yearly best-seller list is Faith Baldwin, who published close to one hundred novels between 1921 and 1977. Stanley J. Kunitz and Howard Haycraft assert in *Twentieth-Century Authors* (1942) that Baldwin "now ranks next to Kathleen Norris [one of the most popular best-selling writers of the period] in her field, both in prolificness and in financial returns." (65) One year after Baldwin's death in 1978, another biographer pointed to the writer's "enormous popular and financial success." (Thiebaux 1979, 444) Given Baldwin's appeal to—literally—generations of women readers and given the fact that Baldwin explores the difficulties of combining marriage and career more frequently than most other popular woman writers of the era, several Faith Baldwin novels have been examined in the chapter on women and work.

6. Lofroth suggests that popular fiction in general supports a conservative social perspective. He writes that the "final resolution [of popular literature] would appear always to be a reaffirmation of the status quo." (1983, 13)

CHAPTER 1: THE FLAPPER AND HER SISTERS

1. Fass concludes that, "[a]lthough mating choices, sexual expression, and cultural forms had been newly tuned to an emerging American life style, they were still very much within the main line of the culture." (1977, 366)

2. In her study of spectatorship in the silent film era, Miriam Hansen observes that as a male sexual object for females, Valentino held a "position that patriarchal tradition usually reserved for the woman." (1991, 260)

3. For further information regarding Julia Peterkin's life and work, see Thomas H. Landers, *Julia Peterkin* (Boston: Twayne, 1976).

4. For an analysis of this film, see Jonathan Rosenbaum, "Gold Diggers of 1953: Howard Hawks' *Gentlemen Prefer Blondes*," *Sight & Sound* 54 (Winter 1984/85), 45–49. See also Lucie Arbuthnot and Gail Seneca, "Pre-Text and Text in *Gentlemen Prefer Blondes*," in *Issues in Feminist Film Criticism*, edited by Patricia Erens, 112–25 (Bloomington: Indiana University Press); and Maureen Turim, "Gentlemen Consume Blondes," also in *Issues in Feminist Film Criticism*, 101–11.

5. In *A Very Serious Thing* (1988) Nancy Walker presents a somewhat different interpretation of the novel, suggesting that it is a satire rather than a farce. Thus, Walker contends that Loos is attempting to subvert existing stereotypes of women rather than merely trying to poke fun at them.

6. See Bertrand F. Richards, *Gene Stratton-Porter* (Boston: Twayne, 1980), and Judith Reick Long, *Gene Stratton-Porter: Novelist and Naturalist* (Bloomington: Indiana University Press, 1990) for background on Stratton-Porter's life and work.

7. Given the fact that the protagonists of Stratton-Porter's best-known books— *Freckles* (1904), *A Girl of the Limberlost* (1909), and *Laddie* (1913)—are children or adolescents, one might argue that Stratton-Porter's work is aimed at children rather than at adult women. Although two of her collections of stories, *After the Flood* (1911) and *Morning Face* (1916), were written explicitly for children, it seems clear that all of her novels were intended for an adult readership. Three of her books were serialized in *McCall's*, a magazine which catered to a middle-class adult female audience, and her biographer points out that she "was published consistently and simultaneously" in both *McCall's* and *Good Housekeeping*. (Richards 1980, 125) While some of Stratton-Porter's novels appear to be fictionalized accounts of her childhood—and earned her the reputation of being the writer of "nothing but sugary romances and molasses fiction" (Richards 1980, 87), other books deal with problems besetting more mature characters, such as the "love-triangle" which drives the plot of *At the Foot of the Rainbow* (1907) or the greed, bankruptcy, illegitimacy, suicide, and dementia which bedevil the characters in *The White Flag* (1923).

8. See Fass (1977, 262–76) for a discussion of the sexual behavior of young women in the Twenties.

CHAPTER 2: MARRIED WOMEN

1. For further information regarding Dorothy Canfield Fisher's life and works, see Dorothy H. Washington, *Dorothy Canfield Fisher: A Biography* (Shelburne, VT: New England Press, 1982).

2. For further information regarding Susan Glaspell's life and works, see Arthur E. Waterman, *Susan Glaspell* (New York: Twayne, 1966).

3. A more famous Glaspell work, of course, than *Ambrose Holt and Family* (1931) is the author's one-act play entitled "Trifles" (1916), the short-story adaptation of which is called "A Jury of Her Peers." This piece is as much an attack on "marriage as usual" as is the later novel. In "Trifles," we learn that Minnie Wright's domineering husband has destroyed his wife's sense of self, just as he has literally killed her canary. Sensitive to the constraints of being women in a patriarchal society, it is the wives of the sheriff and a neighbor who piece together the evidence and conclude that Minnie Wright had finally had enough. When Wright choked Minnie's bird, she strangled him.

For further analyses of this work, see Judith Fetterley, "Reading about Reading: 'A Jury of Her Peers,' 'The Murders in the Rue Morgue,' and 'The Yellow Wallpaper,'" in *Gender and Reading: Essays on Readers, Texts, and Contexts*, edited by Elizabeth A. Flynn and Patrocinio P. Schweickart, 147–64 (Baltimore: Johns Hopkins University Press, 1986); and Sandra M. Gilbert and Susan Gubar, *No Man's Land: The Place of the Woman Writer in the Twentieth Century, Volume I* (New Haven, CT: Yale, 1988): 90–91.

4. It may not have been Wharton's appeal to their readers that prompted these magazine editors to pay top dollar for a Wharton story or novel. When Wharton once asked Rutger B. Jewett, her editor at Appleton who also served as her unofficial agent, why her work was in demand among the mass-circulation magazines, Jewett replied that it was the advertisers who wanted it. "They won't pay top-notch rates . . . unless they're *enclosed in an Edith Wharton or a Galsworthy story*!!! Now beat that." (Lewis 1975, 484) Wharton herself welcomed the higher prices the American picture magazines paid her, but she regarded the magazines themselves with a certain disdain. After a series of set-tos with various popular magazines in the Thirties, Wharton concluded to Jewett, "I am afraid that I cannot write down to the present standards of the American picture magazines." (Lewis 1975, 507) One assumes that Wharton essentially shared Jewett's assessment of the mass-market magazines when he wrote her that "[w]ork of high literary quality . . . is not so good for these popular magazines as the typical lowbrow serial publication. Mary Roberts Rinehart and Kathleen Norris grind out ideal stuff—for serialization. You write novels without a thought for the magazine." (Lewis 1975, 472) It is true that the average reader of a Wharton novel—whether serialized in a magazine or published in book form—may not have fully appreciated Wharton's irony or her technical skill, but she may have identified with the characters and their predicaments.

5. See Julie Olin-Ammentorp's discussion of Selden in "Edith Wharton's Challenge to Feminist Criticism." (1988, 240)

CHAPTER 3: DIVORCED WOMEN

1. Wharton is not sympathetic toward the flappers of the Twenties. As Ammons writes, "Flappers appear in other Wharton novels [besides *The Children*] set in the 1920s—Lilla Gates in *The Mother's Recompense* and Lita Wyant in *Twilight Sleep*—and the author obviously dislikes both. She makes them ignorant, selfish, trivial, promiscuous, careless, and, above all, childish. For despite her semblance of

autonomy, the flapper as Wharton presents her only superficially defies the old ideal of docile femininity. Pleasing men remains her object in life; she is not really independent or self-determining." (1980, 179)

2. For further information regarding Margaret Ayer Barnes' life and works, see Lloyd C. Taylor, *Margaret Ayer Barnes* (New York: Twayne, 1974).

3. Cicily insists that her young husband Jack become a banker in her father's firm, even though he would prefer to go to Boston Tech and study engineering. When her twins are born, she leaves them with the nurse most of the time while she is out in her roadster; she isn't even concerned when her babies are sick, saying it is the doctor's job to cure them. When Cecily decides to leave her husband for Albert Lancaster, she appears to be selfishly sacrificing the stability of her family to achieve her personal happiness.

CHAPTER 4: WOMEN AT WORK

1. If Dot, on the one hand, is anxious to be busier with childcare and housework; Evangeline Knapp in Canfield's *The Home-Maker* (1924), on the other hand, feels trapped in a never-ending routine of domestic chores. She reluctantly declines the minister's offer of a committee chairmanship, asserting "I have too much to do at home. It's all I can manage to get to church and to [church] Guild meeting once a week. I never leave the house for anything else except to go to market." (62) How much work did homemaking require by the Twenties and Thirties? For many wives of the period, traditional domestic chores were beginning to occupy less and less time. Middle-class couples were having fewer children. Housewives were able to take advantage of new labor-saving devices, such as automatic washing machines, electric vacuum cleaners, and refrigerators. Women bought ready-made clothing and processed foods in greater quantity than ever before. Scholars, however, are divided in their judgments as to whether or not these domestic changes actually ushered in a new, more leisured era for the middle-class home-maker. Many social historians have argued that these timesaving trends were offset by a change in the nature of women's domestic responsibilities. Women may have had fewer children, but they were increasingly expected to spend more "quality time" with their offspring, to monitor and shape their children's physical, psychological, intellectual, and moral development—with the help of a battery of experts: "the psychologist, the pediatrician, the child guidance clinic, and the nursery school." (Brown 1987, 121) Women may have found cleaning, cooking, and washing easier, but they often discovered that their housekeeping chores were no less time-consuming. Once the use of washing machines and vacuum cleaners became widespread, standards of cleanliness rose: shirts and underwear were to be washed after each wearing, not once a week. Instead of setting aside one day a week as washday, women found themselves filling and emptying their washing machines continually. Women may have begun to buy more processed foods and ready-made clothing, but at the same time they found their primary role as producer of household goods being replaced by a new role as consumer. By the 1920s, shopping had become a major part of the housewife's activities. And the effort to purchase the best products at the lowest prices proved to be time-consuming indeed. Of the best-selling novels reviewed for this study, only the farm and pioneer novels describe the workday in any detail. With the notable exception of

Canfield's *The Squirrel-Cage* (1912), *The Home-Maker* (1924), and *Her Son's Wife* (1926), those popular novels set in the urban present pay relatively little attention to home work; thus, they say little about the broad changes in homemaking taking place at this time. For further information regarding the history of homemaking, see Susan Strasser, *Never Done: A History of American Housework* (1982).

During this period, leisure-time activities were undergoing changes as fundamental as those taking place in work carried out at home or in the factory. Popular culture was becoming increasingly organized, mechanized, and commercialized. Professional sports teams were formed, urban amusement parks opened, and cycling clubs proliferated in cities across the country. More and more, people were becoming passive consumers of mass-produced and mass-distributed forms of popular culture—as radio-listeners, moviegoers, and readers of confession magazines and newspaper comic strips. For further information regarding changes in popular culture, see John Kasson, *Amusing the Million: Coney Island at the Turn of the Century* (New York: Hill & Wang, 1978); Roy Rosenzweig, *Eight Hours for What We Will: Workers & Leisure in an Industrial City, 1870–1920* (New York: Cambridge University Press, 1983); Kathy Peiss, *Cheap Amusements: Working Women and Leisure in Turn-of-the-Century New York* (Philadelphia: Temple University Press, 1986); and Richard Butsch, editor, *For Fun and Profit: The Transformation of Leisure into Consumption* (Philadelphia: Temple University Press, 1990). In general, these developments in leisure-time activities are no more reflected in the popular novels of the day than are changes in domestic labor. Popular novelists tend to show their characters engaging in relatively traditional types of social activities. They attend dances and picnics; they go to concerts and plays; they hold dinners, take walks and visit friends.

Those who engage in other types of leisure-time activities seem to be doing so only to occupy an idle hour in an aimless life. In Faith Baldwin's *"Something Special,"* (1940), wealthy socialite Andrea Meredith dabbles in a succession of hobbies—painting, ceramics, welfare committee work, theater—and discards them each in turn. In Edith Wharton's *Twilight Sleep* (1927), Pauline Manford devotes herself to eurythmic exercises, manicures and massages, dancing lessons, and committee work. Edna Jones, in Margaret Ayer Barnes' *Edna His Wife* (1935), relies upon movies and women's magazines to fill her days. She reads the *Ladies' Home Journal* from cover to cover—"its stories, its illustrations, its household hints, its beauty columns, its advertisements, even the disconnected chapters of its two serials." (367) Edna, who appears to have married her husband primarily because he reminded her of the man in the Gibson Girl illustrations, retreats further and further from the painful reality of her loveless marriage into the unrealistic world of Hollywood movies, savoring the romance of matinee idols, whose courtships end in blissful marriages with none of the tensions and disappointments of her own.

CHAPTER 5: FARMING AND PIONEER WOMEN

1. Cather's portrayal of Alexandra in this regard is consistent with what Carol Fairbanks has found to be typical of other prairie women novelists' treatments of their heroines. In *Prairie Women: Images in American and Canadian Fiction* (1986), Fairbanks argues that it is generally a male assumption that the "land must be

subdued; in subduing the land a person becomes heroic. . . . Women writing in the tradition of prairie women's fiction generally insist on women's heroism arising out of their ability to work *with* the land." (170)

In Cather biographer Sharon O'Brien's view, Alexandra is a mixture of masculine and feminine attributes, possessing "the seemingly contradictory traits American society divides between men and women—strength and pragmatism as well as intuition and compassion." (1987, 429) Only such a person, Cather suggests, could have compelled the prairie to "bend" to her will. "Significantly," Cather scholar Susan J. Rosowski writes, "Alexandra awakens a female principle of active receptivity in the land." (1981, 263) Under Alexandra's sensitive management, the prairie blossoms.

2. One should not, however, overemphasize this point. It is worth noting that the women characters discussed here are all farmers, an occupation traditionally carried on by females upon the death of a husband or father. As we saw in the previous chapter, women are only infrequently shown to enter non-farm occupations—much less to achieve success in such endeavors.

3. While Lillian Schlissel and Annette Kolodny claim that women's letters and diaries indicate that females seldom were the ones to choose to relocate to the frontier and were often initially unhappy at the prospect of such an undertaking, Sandra Myres argues that the written record suggests that women were as eager to move West as were their husbands, as both women and men read the same "positive and optimistic" booster accounts of the wilderness. (Schlissel 1982; Kolodny 1984; Myres 1982, 16)

4. Diony Hall, in Elizabeth Madox Roberts' *The Great Meadow* (1930), and Sabra Cravat, in Edna Ferber's *Cimarron* (1929), are equally unwilling to move West; it is their husbands who elect to do so. Once they arrive at their destinations, however, they throw themselves wholeheartedly into their new roles as frontierswomen, and they find themselves as equal to the hardships and perils of the wilderness as Abbie Deal.

5. Like Abbie Deal, Diony Hall in *The Great Meadow* seeks to civilize the wilderness. She has a "vision of sheep sprinkled over a pasture . . . of stone walls and rail fences setting bounds to the land . . . of neighbors . . . each in his own land, their children meeting together to walk down the road to a schoolhouse or a church." (Roberts 1930, 208–9) In *The Great Meadow*, as in *A Lantern in Her Hand* (1928), both sexes alike look forward to the time in which a new society will take form. When Berk first tries to persuade Diony to travel West to Kentucky with him, it is he who speaks of starting a "new world there." (Roberts 1930, 118) In this book, in contrast to Aldrich's novel, it seems to be the women, like Diony, who can most vividly picture the future in their mind's eye, who most clearly foresee the "beginning before the beginning." (Roberts 1930, 207)

6. While Diony Hall Jarvis and Abbie Deal are both vital participants in the creation of a new Eden, Sabra Cravat instead stands accused by her creator of being a destroyer of "the Second Paradise." (Myres 1982, 3) In Ferber's *Cimarron* (1929), Sabra's husband Yancey decides to settle in the newly opened Oklahoma Territory, and, from the first, Sabra is appalled by the lack of polish and refinement of her new surroundings. "Grimly," Ferber writes, "Sabra (and, in time, the other virtuous women of the community) set about making this new frontier town like the old as speedily as possible" (166), while Yancey fights a losing battle to keep

the new unchanged. It is clear that Ferber's sympathies lie with Yancey. However, the "deadliest shot in all the deadly shooting Southwest" (102), befriender of Indians and of good-hearted prostitutes, Yancey Cravat is no match for his wife and her female allies. By the end of the novel, Yancey's West is gone and Yancey himself is reduced to a "picturesque character" (335) with one last quixotic gesture left to make. In *Cimarron*, Sabra Cravat may be the "civilizing woman," but Ferber questions the value of such activity. As Myres observes, the stereotype of the civilizing frontier woman has had negative as well as positive connotations. "The arrival of the gentle tamers in the wilderness," Myres writes, "also curtailed male freedom and forced unwanted control upon men's self-imposed rejection of civilized values." (1982, 3) Sabra Cravat is a "petticoat pioneer" like Mollie Wood in Owen Wister's *The Virginian*, who has brought "law and order, cleanliness, and religion" to a region which was previously a "fine, free, male place." (Myres 1982, 3–4)

7. Carroll was not the only woman novelist of the Thirties to assert that farmers should rely on their own initiative and not on government help to overcome their difficulties. As Anita Clair Fellman has noted in a study of Laura Ingalls Wilder and her daughter Rose Wilder Lane, Lane later claimed that her mother "specifically intended the [Little House] series to be a criticism of the New Deal" (1990, 558)—and an affirmation of individualism and self-sufficiency. Lane's *Let the Hurricane Roar* (1933), first published in the *Saturday Evening Post* and then in book form, inspired a *Post* editorial "reminding its readers that surely the dominant American national trait was self-reliance and warning them that the growth of government was undermining their self-reliance." (Fellman 1990, 552) Fellman sees both Wilder and Lane as being "predisposed . . . to a perception of the solitary individual as the true social unit and to a belief in political individualism." (Fellman 1990, 560)

8. See Fairbanks 1986, 12–21.

9. In an afterword to the 1991 reprint, Nancy Hoffman also suggests that *Now in November* (1934) is organized in both cyclical and linear time. Yet, Hoffman posits that Johnson conceives of "[s]easonal patterns [that] continue on into infinity" (241) while I would suggest that, whatever seasonal progression is to come, the narrator will remain trapped in a November of the spirit.

10. Hoffman argues that nature does have a "sustaining and healing" power in the novel. (1991, 253) I would disagree. Although the narrator does find refuge in the woods in times of trouble, and at such times "the woods seemed all answer and healing and more than enough to live for," nature cannot completely erase her anxieties. After all, she thinks that "maybe they [the woods] wouldn't always be ours—that a drouth or a too-wet year or even a year over-good when everyone else had too much to sell—could snatch them away from us, and a scratch on a piece of paper could cancel a hundred acres and all our lives. And this same sick fear came up again like a sly and smothering hand." (Johnson 1934, 68) Near the end of the book, when Marget is beset by new crises, she again finds that "[o]nly by getting away from the house and off in the fields sometimes could I keep sane and find life bearable." (Johnson 1934, 215) But even now nature provides only partial relief: "It was not a healing; —neither from earth nor love nor from any one thing alone comes healing,—but without this I should have died." (Johnson 1934, 215–16)

CHAPTER 6: SACRIFICIAL HEROINES

1. If most middle-class women used cosmetics sparingly, to achieve a "natural" look, flappers used cosmetics more boldly. To call attention to the use of beauty products may be more honest than to employ them more circumspectly—while claiming to admire only unmediated beauty. In fact, young women's open use of cosmetics in the Twenties may have been an act of assertion: by emphasizing female sexuality through the application of exotic shades of lipstick and nail polish, women may have been challenging the traditional gender definition of women as modest and asexual. This was not, of course, the way that popular novelists like Bailey and Norris "read" such behavior.

2. In Dorothy Canfield's *Her Son's Wife* (1926), Mary Bascomb is shocked when her only son Ralph brings home his new bride. The older woman regards Lottie as "common" and self-centered. Mrs. Bascomb finds Lottie to be a hopeless house-keeper, but, six months after the couple has moved in with her, she discovers that Lottie is even worse as a mother. Lottie makes no attempt to keep the baby's clothes clean, ignores the child while she entertains a "man friend" in the living room, and becomes possessive toward little "Dids" only when she wishes to spite her mother-in-law.

Although Lottie appears at first to fit the standard profile of the antiheroine, her characterization is more complex than this. As the novel progresses, we learn that Lottie herself received a poor upbringing. Lottie's dying father confesses to Mrs. Bascomb, "She never had no chance, my poor girl hadn't. If she'd a-ben looked out for, the way you've looked out for Dids. . . . But we didn't know no better, her mother and me." (283) By the end of the novel, Mrs. Bascomb's attitude toward her son's wife has changed from contempt to compassion. Mary Bascomb sees Lottie in a new light, as a "forlorn little phantom, a helpless desolate child . . . doomed from the hour she drew breath, ignorant, unprotected, warped, stunted." (288) As Dids leaves for college, Mrs. Bascomb realizes that her task of raising her grand-daughter may be ending but the job of mothering Lottie is just beginning.

3. In *Her Son's Wife* Canfield suggests that there is a right and a wrong way to go about "doing one's duty." At first, the proper and respectable Mrs. Bascomb grimly suffers the indignity of sharing her house with her son and his "cheap, ignorant, vulgar" wife. (45) The older woman "shut herself up in a self-contained fury of silent martyrdom and hard work. . . . She accepted in a rock-like silence Lottie's enormities as a house companion." (52) It is not until Mrs. Bascomb is able to submerge her sense of self and to accept her son and his wife as they are that she is able to become a more compassionate and truly virtuous person.

4. In 1990 it was remade as a star vehicle for Bette Midler.

5. King Vidor, perhaps more consciously and in a more complex way than Prouty, manipulates our notions of class. The questions of class raised by the 1937 film are not easy to resolve. As Wendy Lesser observes in *His Other Half: Men Looking at Women through Art* (Cambridge, MA: Harvard University Press, 1991), we are led to believe that Barbara Stanwyck, as Stella, is making the right decision when she stands aside so that her daughter can ascend into upper-class society; yet, Lesser notes, "one of Vidor's more obvious points would seem to be that typing by class is an insufficient way to see people." (230) We may identify with the upper-class characters in the film when they laugh at Stella's "working-class

accent, at her increasingly overdone outfits, her loud, unrefined voice, and her forceful, unladylike walk" (229); but we also see these well-bred characters as colorless and overly refined. In contrast, Stella emerges as the most vibrant, genuine, and generous character in the film. Despite her uncouth behavior, she has a strength and humanity which the "better" characters lack.

In *American Film Melodrama* (1989), Robert Lang makes a similar point regarding the ambiguity of class in this film. "Society—bourgeois ideology itself—is the villain," Lang writes, "even though its ideal as represented by Stephen and the Morrisons is not unattractive. Stella, the film's heroine and chief figure for audience identification, is likeable, warm, earthy, generous."(151) Yet, Lang argues, Stella must effect her own "repression/oppression" (152) by sacrificing her daughter in the name of "patriarchal ideology" in order to bring the film to a satisfying conclusion.

For other analyses of the 1937 film, see Mary Ann Doane, *The Desire to Desire: The Woman's Film of the 1940s* (Bloomington: Indiana University Press, 1987); E. Ann Kaplan, "The Case of the Missing Mother: Maternal Issues in Vidor's Stella Dallas," *Heresies* 16 (1983): 81–85; and Linda Williams, " 'Something Else Besides a Mother': Stella Dallas and the Maternal Melodrama," *Cinema Journal* 24 (1984): 2–27.

6. According to Ellen Serlen Uffen, *Back Street's* (1931) popularity was due to three factors: (1) it was published during the Depression, when "escapist entertainment" was particularly welcome, (2) it dealt with the "especially titillating subject of sex," and (3) readers, "perhaps recalling similar trials," empathized with Ray Schmidt. (1979, 362) It is hard to regard Ray's tragic plight as particularly escapist, and Hurst's treatment of sex in this novel is hardly titillating. On the other hand, many readers may have believed that they were sacrificing themselves for the sake of husbands or children who were not sufficiently grateful to them. Occasionally they may even have doubted that the objects of their devotion were worthy of their generosity. Thus, readers may well have identified with Ray Schmidt and her predicament.

7. In Rachel Field's *Time Out of Mind* (1935), Kate Furnald makes an equally great sacrifice for the man she loves. When Kate's mother becomes housekeeper at Fortune's Folly, Kate grows up with the two Fortune children and eventually falls in love with Nat Fortune. Kate becomes engaged to an ambitious fisherman from a nearby village, who resents Kate's friendship with the socially prominent Fortunes. Kate breaks her engagement and later sacrifices her reputation for Nat, and Nat, unlike Hurst's Walter Saxel, seems worthy of Kate's devotion. He is a talented symphony composer who needs the tranquility only Kate can provide in order to work. When he marries a woman who is more interested in his social status than in his music, his career and his health suffer. He retreats to Fortune's Folly and to Kate and begins to recover under her care, but her love cannot save him from decline and death caused by the nervous debility which has plagued him from childhood.

8. In her analysis of *Rebecca* (1938), Sally Beauman offers a different interpretation. Beauman concedes that "[o]ne way of reading 'Rebecca' is as a love story, in which the good woman triumphs over the bad by winning a man's love . . . a reading that undoubtedly helped make 'Rebecca' a best-seller." (Beauman 1993, 133) However, Beauman argues, du Maurier has actually written a darker tale than

commonly recognized. The second Mrs. de Winter does not live "happily ever after" at the end of the novel: "[f]ollowing him [her husband] into that hellish exile glimpsed at the beginning, she becomes again what she was when she met him—a paid companion to a tyrant. For humoring his whims and obeying his dictates, her recompense this time is love, not money, and the cost is her identity." (Beauman 1993, 134) While du Maurier may well have intended to subvert the conventions of the romance genre by providing an unhappy ending, Beauman herself acknowledges that few readers or critics read *Rebecca* in this way at the time of its publication.

9. In his introduction to the anniversary edition of *Gone with the Wind*, published in 1975, novelist James Michener also described the novel's popularity:

It is difficult even now to comprehend what a staggering event *Gone with the Wind* was in that post-depression year of 1936. . . . So great was the word-of-mouth publicity . . . that within twenty days of publication 176,000 copies had been sold. Over the summer months, when bookstores customarily fell into doldrums, sales rose to 700,000 copies, one New York store ordering 50,000 on one day. Within a year of publication, 1,383,000 copies had been sold. Today, sales stand at about 21,000,000. (71–72)

10. Pyron reports that a psychiatrist classified Scarlett as a "partial psychopath," who "fails regularly to respond to sincere emotion in her lovers and pursues above all else aims that are fundamentally egocentric and trivial." (1991, 257)According to Pyron, Mitchell was delighted with Dr. Hervey Cleckley's diagnosis, and she wrote him to tell him so.

11. Given the epic scope of the novel, with its multitude of characters and its interweaving of personal and public drama, *Gone with the Wind* (1936) is closer in type to the "Reconstruction romance" or "plantation romance" of the late nineteenth and early twentieth century represented by the works of Thomas Nelson Page or Thomas Dixon than it is to the woman's romance exemplified in the novels of Temple Bailey or Kathleen Norris. "On the surface," as Kenneth O'Brien points out," there is much in *Gone with the Wind* that is perfectly consistent with the scenes, stock types, and literary forms used by Page." (1983, 157) Nevertheless, Scarlett O'Hara is no more the typical heroine of this genre than she is of the woman's romance genre. A common plot device in the Reconstruction romance is the rape of the innocent white heroine by a savage black assailant, an act which is used, in Thomas Dixon's *The Clansman*, for example, to justify the rise of the Klan. In *Gone with the Wind*, Scarlett is nearly raped, but Mitchell tells us that it is her heroine's willful disregard for her own safety which has precipitated the attack: "in an extraordinary departure from tradition," O'Brien writes, "the 'victim' herself becomes responsible for the attack." (161) Scarlett's insistence upon maintaining her independence, in this episode and in others, indicates that she is unwilling to accept the role that society expects of her. O'Brien concludes that Mitchell's "exploration of the myth of Southern womanhood . . . make[s] *Gone with the Wind* profoundly different from anything in the older tradition" of the Reconstruction romance. (166)

12. We know quite a bit about contemporary critics' reactions to the characters in this novel, but we have less information about the reactions of contemporary readers. Taylor, who has been cited several times previously, is one of the few scholars to examine reader response to *Gone with the Wind*. Taylor notes that a 1957

survey of American high-school students disclosed that "all but one [of the girls] chose Melanie" over Scarlett as the character with whom they most identified. (1989, 78) A 1970 survey, however, indicated that the tide had begun to turn: "this time three-quarters of the girls named Scarlett" over Melanie. (1989, 78) Based upon the results of her sample, Taylor finds that the "vast majority" of contemporary readers and viewers regard Scarlett O'Hara as their "favourite character." (1989, 78) It is unfortunate that no systematic survey of readers' attitudes was undertaken when the book was first published, although a quantitative analysis of the thousands of letters Mitchell received from readers could provide useful evidence regarding reader response to Scarlett and Melanie.

CONCLUSION

1. A representative of Amereon House informed me that the bulk of their orders for early twentieth-century popular novels comes from elderly customers who want to reread the books that they enjoyed when they were younger, or who want to purchase the books to give to their grandchildren.

Selected Bibliography

WOMEN'S NOVELS CITED

Aldrich, Bess Streeter (1928). *A Lantern in Her Hand*. Reprint. New York: D. Appleton-Century Company, 1934.

_____ (1933). *Miss Bishop*. Reprint. Lincoln: University of Nebraska Press, 1960.

_____ (1935). *Spring Came On Forever*. New York: D. Appleton-Century Company.

_____ (1931). *A White Bird Flying*. New York: D. Appleton & Company.

Atherton, Gertrude (1923). *Black Oxen*. New York: Boni & Liveright.

Bailey, Temple (1926). *The Blue Window*. New York: Grosset & Dunlap.

_____ (1923). *The Dim Lantern*. New York: Grosset & Dunlap.

_____ (1932). *Little Girl Lost*. Philadelphia: The Penn Publishing Company.

_____ (1924). *Peacock Feathers*. New York: Grosset & Dunlap.

_____ (1928). *Silver Slippers*. New York: Grosset & Dunlap.

_____ (1927). *Wallflowers*. Philadelphia: The Penn Publishing Company.

Baldwin, Faith (1928). *Alimony*. Reprint. New York: Triangle Press, 1943.

_____ (1930). *The Office Wife*. Reprint. Philadelphia: Blakiston Company, 1945.

_____ (1940). *"Something Special."* Reprint. Philadelphia: Blakiston Company, 1946.

_____ (1932). *Week-End Marriage*. Reprint. Philadelphia: Blakiston Company, 1944.

_____ (1933). *White Collar Girl*. New York: Farrar & Rinehart.

Barnes, Margaret Ayer (1935). *Edna His Wife*. Boston: Houghton Mifflin.

_____ (1931). *Westward Passage*. Boston: Houghton Mifflin.

_____ (1938). *Wisdom's Gate*. Boston: Houghton Mifflin.

_____ (1933). *Within This Present*. Boston: Houghton Mifflin.

_____ (1930). *Years of Grace*. Boston: Houghton Mifflin.

Brush, Katharine (1930). *Young Man of Manhattan*. Murray Hill, NY: Farrar & Rinehart.

Buck, Pearl S. (1931). *The Good Earth*. New York: Thomas Y. Crowell.

Canfield, Dorothy (1915). *The Bent Twig*. New York: Grosset & Dunlap.

_____ (1921). *The Brimming Cup*. New York: Harcourt, Brace & Company.

_____ (1926). *Her Son's Wife*. New York: Harcourt, Brace & Company.

_____ (1924). *The Home-Maker*. Reprint. Chicago: Academy Chicago, 1983.

_____ (1912). *The Squirrel-Cage*. New York: Grosset & Dunlap.

Carroll, Gladys Hasty (1933). *As the Earth Turns*. New York: Macmillan Company.

_____ (1935). *A Few Foolish Ones*. New York: Macmillan Company.

Cather, Willa (1918). *My Antonia*. Boston: Houghton Mifflin.

_____ (1913). *O Pioneers!* Boston: Houghton Mifflin.

Chase, Mary Ellen (1934). *Mary Peters*. New York: Macmillan Company.

Delmar, Vina (1928). *Bad Girl*. New York: Harcourt, Brace & Company.

DuMaurier, Daphne (1938). *Rebecca*. Reprint. New York: Avon Books, 1971.

Fairbank, Janet Ayer (1936). *Rich Man, Poor Man*. Boston: Houghton Mifflin.

Ferber, Edna (1929). *Cimarron*. Garden City, NY: Doubleday & Co.

_____ (1926). *Show Boat*. Garden City, NY: Doubleday & Co.

_____ (1924). *So Big*. Garden City, NY: Doubleday, Page & Co.

Field, Rachel (1938). *All This, and Heaven Too*. New York: Macmillan.

_____ (1935). *Time Out of Mind*. Reprint. New York: Macmillan, 1947.

Gale, Zona (1923). *Faint Perfume*. New York: D. Appleton and Company.

_____ (1920). *Miss Lulu Bett*. New York: Grosset & Dunlap.

Glasgow, Ellen (1925). *Barren Ground*. Reprint. New York: Sagamore Press, 1957.

_____ (1935). *Vein of Iron*. New York: Harcourt, Brace & Company.

Glaspell, Susan (1931). *Ambrose Holt and Family*. New York: Frederick A. Stokes Company.

_____ (1916). "Trifles." In *The Norton Anthology of Literature by Women: The Tradition in English*, compiled by Sandra M. Gilbert and Susan Gubar, 1st edition, 1139–1399. New York: Norton, 1985.

Glyn, Elinor (1907). *Three Weeks*. New York: Duffield.

Hull, E. M. (1921). *The Sheik*. Boston: Small, Maynard & Company.

Hurst, Fannie (1931). *Back Street*. New York: Grosset & Dunlap.

_____ (1933). *Imitation of Life*. Reprint. New York: Harper & Row, 1990.

_____ (1923). *Lummox*. New York: P. F. Collier & Son.

Johnson, Josephine (1934). *Now in November*. New York: Simon and Schuster.

Lane, Rose Wilder (1938). *Free Land*. New York: Longmans, Green and Company.

_____ (1933). *Let the Hurricane Roar*. New York: Longmans, Green and Company.

Loos, Anita (1977). *Cast of Thousands*. New York: Grosset & Dunlap.

_____ (1925). "Gentlemen Prefer Blondes." Reprint. New York: Liveright Publishing Company, 1963.

Miller, Caroline (1933). *Lamb in His Bosom*. New York: Harper & Row.

Mitchell, Margaret (1936). *Gone with the Wind*. New York: Macmillan.

Norris, Kathleen (1936). *The American Flaggs*. Garden City, NY: Doubleday, Doran & Company.

_____ (1929). *Barberry Bush*. Garden City, NY: Doubleday, Doran & Company.

_____ (1929). *Butterfly*. Garden City, NY: Doubleday, Doran & Company.

_____ (1929). *The Foolish Virgin*. Garden City, NY: Doubleday, Doran & Company.

_____ (1920). *Harriet and the Piper*. New York: A. L. Burt Company.

_____ (1916). *The Heart of Rachael*. New York: Grosset & Dunlap.

_____ (1911). *Mother*. New York: Macmillan.

_____ (1925). *Noon: An Autobiographical Sketch*. Garden City, NY: Doubleday, Page & Company.

_____ (1930). *Passion Flower*. Reprint. New York: Paperback Library, 1970.

_____ (1924). *Rose of the World*. New York: Doubleday, Page & Company.

_____ (1927). *The Sea Gull*. Reprint. New York: Paperback Library, 1970.

_____ (1929). *The Story of Julia Page*. Garden City, NY: Doubleday, Doran & Company

Ostenso, Martha (1925). *Wild Geese*. New York: Dodd, Mead & Company.

Parrott, Ursula (1929). *Ex-Wife*. Reprint. New York: New American Library, 1989.

Peterkin, Julia (1928). *Scarlet Sister Mary*. Indianapolis: Bobbs-Merrill.

Prouty, Olive Higgins (1923). *Stella Dallas*. Reprint. New York: Perennial Library, 1990.

Rinehart, Mary Roberts (1934). *The State versus Elinor Norton*. New York: Farrar & Rinehart.

Roberts, Elizabeth Madox (1930). *The Great Meadow*. New York: Literary Guild.

Stratton-Porter, Gene (1918). *A Daughter of the Land*. Garden City, NY: Doubleday, Page & Company.

_____ (1909). *A Girl of the Limberlost*. New York: Grosset & Dunlap.

_____ (1921). *Her Father's Daughter*. New York: Grosset & Dunlap.

Turnbull, Agnes Sligh (1936). *The Rolling Years*. New York: Macmillan.

Wharton, Edith (1920). *The Age of Innocence*. Reprint. New York: Signet, 1962.

_____ (1911). "Autres Temps . . ." In *Roman Fever and Other Stories*, 235–76. New York: Collier Books, 1987.

_____ (1913). *The Custom of the Country*. New York: Charles Scribner's Sons.

_____ (1922). *The Glimpses of the Moon*. New York: Appleton.

_____ (1905). *The House of Mirth*. New York: Charles Scribner's Sons.

_____ (1925). *The Mother's Recompense*. Reprint. New York: Charles Scribner's Sons, 1986.

_____ (1904). "The Other Two." In *The Norton Anthology of Literature by Women: The Tradition in English*, compiled by Sandra M. Gilbert and Susan Gubar, 1st edition, 1184–99. New York: Norton, 1985.

_____ (1927). *Twilight Sleep*. New York: D. Appleton & Company.

Wilder, Laura Ingalls (1932). *Little House in the Big Woods*. Reprint. Harper & Row, 1953.

_____ (1935). *Little House on the Prairie*. New York: Harper & Brothers.

SECONDARY WORKS CITED

Ammons, Elizabeth (1980). *Edith Wharton's Argument with America*. Athens: University of Georgia Press.

Anderson, Rachel (1974). *The Purple Heart Throbs: The Sub-Literature of Love*. London: Hodder & Stoughton.

Auchincloss, Louis (1962). "Foreword." To *The Age of Innocence* by Edith Wharton, v–xi. Reprint. New York: Signet.

Bakerman, Jane S. (1979). "Gene Stratton-Porter." In *American Women Writers: A Critical Reference Guide from Colonial Times to the Present*, edited by Lina Mainiero, Vol. 4, 443–46. New York: Frederick Ungar.

Banner, Lois (1983). *American Beauty*. New York: Alfred A. Knopf.

Barnett, James Harwood (1939). *Divorce and the American Divorce Novel, 1858–1937: A Study in Literary Reflections of Social Influences*. Reprint. New York: Russell & Russell, 1968.

Beauman, Nicola (1983). *A Very Great Profession: The Woman's Novel, 1914–39*. London: Virago.

Beauman, Sally (1993). "Rereading Rebecca." *New Yorker* (November 8): 127–38.

Bodnar, John (1992). *Remaking America: Public Memory, Commemoration, and Patriotism in the Twentieth Century*. Princeton: Princeton University Press.

Brown, Dorothy M. (1987). *Setting a Course: American Women in the 1920s*. Boston: Twayne.

Brownlow, Kevin (1990). *Behind the Mask of Innocence*. New York: Alfred A. Knopf.

Burnham, John C. (1973). "The Progressive Era Revolution in American Attitudes toward Sex." *Journal of American History* 59 (March): 885–908.

Cawelti, John G. (1976). *Adventure, Mystery, and Romance: Formula Stories as Art and Popular Culture*. Chicago: University of Chicago.

Chafe, William (1972). *The American Woman: Her Changing Social, Economic, and Political Roles, 1920–1970*. Oxford: Oxford University Press.

Cott, Nancy F. (1987). *The Grounding of Modern Feminism*. New Haven, CT: Yale University Press.

Dwyer, Richard (1983). "The Case of the Cool Reception." In *Recasting: Gone with the Wind in American Culture*, edited by Darden Asbury Pyron, 21–31. Miami: University Presses of Florida.

Elson, Ruth Miller (1985). *Myths and Mores in American Best Sellers, 1865–1965*. New York: Garland Publishing.

Fairbanks, Carol (1986). *Prairie Women: Images in American and Canadian Fiction*. New Haven, CT: Yale University Press.

Fass, Paula (1977). *The Damned and the Beautiful: American Youth in the 1920's*. New York: Oxford University Press.

Fellman, Anita Clair (1990). "Laura Ingalls Wilder and Rose Wilder Lane: The Politics of a Mother-Daughter Relationship." *Signs* 15: 535–61.

Fiedler, Leslie A. (1979). *The Inadvertent Epic: From Uncle Tom's Cabin to Roots*. New York: Simon & Schuster.

———— (1966). *Love and Death in the American Novel*. Revised edition. New York: Stein & Day.

Fowler, Bridget (1984). "True to Me Always: An Analysis of Women's Magazine Fiction." In *Popular Fiction and Social Change*, edited by Christopher Pawling, 99–126. London: Macmillan Press.

Fox-Genovese, Elizabeth (1981). "Scarlett O'Hara: The Southern Lady as New Woman." *American Quarterly* 33: 391– 411.

Freedman, Estelle B. (1974). "The New Woman: Changing Views of Women in the 1920's." *Journal of American History* 61 (September): 372–93.

Gittelson, Natalie (1980). "The Packaging of Judith Krantz." *New York Times Magazine* (March 2): 22–31.

Guimond, James (1991). *American Photography and the American Dream*. Chapel Hill: University of North Carolina Press.

Hansen, Miriam (1991). *Babel in Babylon: Spectatorship in American Silent Film*. Cambridge, MA: Harvard University Press.

Hart, James D. (1950). *The Popular Book: A History of America's Literary Taste.* Berkeley: University of California Press.

Harte, Barbara and Carolyn Riley, editors (1969). "Faith Baldwin." In *Contemporary Authors,* Vols. 5–8, 1st revision, 60–61. Detroit: Gale Research Company.

Haskell, Molly (1974). *From Reverence to Rape: The Treatment of Women in the Movies.* New York: Holt, Rinehart & Winston.

Hearn, Charles R. (1977). *The American Dream in the Great Depression.* Westport, CT: Greenwood Press.

Higashi, Sumiko (1979). "Cinderella vs. Statistics: The Silent Movie Heroine as a Jazz-Age Working Girl." In *Woman's Being, Woman's Place,* edited by Mary Kelley, 109–26. Boston: G. K. Hall & Company.

_____ (1978). *Virgins, Vamps, and Flappers: The American Silent Movie Heroine.* Montreal and St. Albans, VT: Eden Press Women's Publications.

Hoffman, Nancy (1991). "Afterword." In *Now in November,* by Josephine Johnson, 235–74. Reprint. New York: Feminist Press.

Hofstadter, Beatrice K. (1978). "Popular Culture and the Romantic Heroine." In *Literary Taste, Culture and Mass Communication: Content and Taste; Religion and Myth,* edited by Peter Davison, Rolf Meyersohn, and Edward Shils, 235–44. Cambridge, England: Chadwyck-Healey.

Honey, Maureen (1990). "Gotham's Daughters: Feminism in the 1920s." *American Studies* 31 (Spring): 25–40.

_____ (1976). "Images of Women in The Saturday Evening Post, 1931–1936." *Journal of Popular Culture* 10 (Fall): 352–58.

_____ (1989). *Shadowed Dreams: Women's Poetry of the Harlem Renaissance.* New Brunswick, NJ: Rutgers University Press.

Jones, Anne Goodwyn (1981). *Tomorrow Is Another Day: The Woman Writer in the South, 1859–1936.* Baton Rouge: Louisiana State University Press.

Katzman, David M. (1978). *Seven Days a Week: Women and Domestic Service in Industrializing America.* New York: Oxford University Press.

Kessler-Harris, Alice (1982). *Out to Work: A History of Wage-Earning Women in the United States.* New York: Oxford University Press.

King, Richard (1983). "The 'Simple Story's' Ideology: Gone with the Wind and the New South Creed." In *Recasting: Gone with the Wind in American Culture,* edited by Darden Asbury Pyron, 167–83. Miami: University Presses of Florida.

Kinsman, Clare D., editor (1975). *Contemporary Authors. Permanent Series.* Detroit: Gale Research Company.

Kolodny, Annette (1984). *The Land Before Her: Fantasy and Experience of the American Frontiers, 1630–1860.* Chapel Hill: University of North Carolina Press.

Kunitz, Stanley J. and Howard Haycraft, editors (1942). *Twentieth-Century Authors: A Biographical Dictionary of Modern Literature.* New York: H. W. Wilson Company.

Lambert, Deborah (1982). "The Defeat of a Hero: Autonomy and Sexuality in My Antonia." *American Literature* 53 (January): 676–90.

Lang, Robert (1989). *American Film Melodrama: Griffith, Vidor, Minnelli.* Princeton: Princeton University Press.

Lawrence, Margaret (1936). *The School of Femininity: A Book For and About Women As They Are Interpreted Through Feminine Writers of Yesterday and Today.* Reprint. Port Washington, NY: Kennikat Press, 1966.

Leuchtenburg, William (1958). *The Perils of Prosperity, 1914–1932*. Chicago: University of Chicago.

Lewis, R.W.B. (1975). *Edith Wharton: A Biography*. New York: Harper & Row.

Lofroth, Erik (1983). *A World Made Safe: Values in American Best Sellers, 1895–1920*. Stockholm: UPPSALA.

Lynd, Robert S. and Helen Merrell Lynd (1929). *Middletown: A Study in Modern American Culture*. New York: Harcourt Brace Jovanovich.

McElvaine, Robert S. (1984). *The Great Depression: America, 1929–1941*. New York: Times Books.

McGovern, James R. (1968). "The American Woman's Pre-World War I Freedom in Manners and Morals." *Journal of American History* 55 (September): 315–33.

Makosky, Donald (1966). "The Portrayal of Women in Wide-Circulation Magazine Short Stories, 1905–1955." Ph.D. diss., University of Pennsylvania.

Marchand, Roland (1985). *Advertising the American Dream: Making Way for Modernity, 1920–1940*. Berkeley: University of California Press.

Marling, Karal Ann (1982). *Wall-to-Wall America: A Cultural History of Post-Office Murals in the Great Depression*. Minneapolis: University of Minnesota Press.

Maslin, Janet (1990). "Shed a Tear for Stella, Still Noble but Senseless." *New York Times* (February 11): II: 15, 18.

May, Elaine Tyler (1980). *Great Expectations: Marriage and Divorce in Post-Victorian America*. Chicago: University of Chicago Press, 1980.

Melosh, Barbara (1991). *Engendering Culture: Manhood and Womanhood in New Deal Public Art and Theater*. Washington: Smithsonian Institution Press.

Meyer, Roy W. (1965). *The Middle Western Farm Novel in the Twentieth Century*. Lincoln: University of Nebraska Press.

Michener, James (1975). "The Company of Giants." Reprinted in *Recasting: Gone with the Wind in American Culture*, edited by Darden Asbury Pyron, 69–97. Miami: University Presses of Florida.

Miner, Madonne M. (1984). *Insatiable Appetites: Twentieth-Century American Women's Bestsellers*. Westport, CT: Greenwood Press.

Mintz, Steven and Susan Kellogg (1988). *Domestic Revolutions: A Social History of American Family Life*. New York: Free Press.

Mussell, Kay (1984). *Fantasy and Reconciliation: Contemporary Formulas of Women's Romance Fiction*. Westport, CT: Greenwood Press.

Myres, Sandra L. (1982). *Westering Women and the Frontier Experience, 1800–1915*. Albuquerque: University of New Mexico Press.

Nye, Russel B. (1970). *The Unembarrassed Muse: The Popular Arts in America*. New York: Dial Press.

O'Brien, Kenneth (1983). "Race, Romance, and the Southern Literary Tradition." In *Recasting: Gone with the Wind in American Culture*, edited by Darden Asbury Pyron, 153–66. Miami: University Presses of Florida.

O'Brien, Sharon (1987). *Willa Cather: The Emerging Voice*. New York: Oxford.

Olin-Ammentorp, Julie (1988). "Edith Wharton's Challenge to Feminist Criticism." *Studies in American Fiction* 16 (Autumn): 237–44.

Overton, Grant (1924). *Cargoes for Crusoes*. New York: D. Appleton.

——— (1928).*The Women Who Make Our Novels*. Reprint. Revised edition. Freeport, NY: Books for Libraries Press, 1967.

Parrott, M. L. (1989). "Afterword" to *Ex-Wife*, by Ursula Parrott, 219–24. Reprint. New York: New American Library.

Prose, Francine (1989). "Introduction" to *Ex-Wife*, by Ursula Parrott, vi-xiv. Reprint. New York: New American Library.

Pyron, Darden Asbury (1991). *Southern Daughter: The Life of Margaret Mitchell*. New York: Oxford University Press.

Rabine, Leslie W. (1985). "Romance in the Age of Electronics: Harlequin Enterprises." *Feminist Studies* 11 (Spring): 39–60.

Radway, Janice A. (1984). *Reading the Romance: Women, Patriarchy and Popular Literature*. Chapel Hill: University of North Carolina Press.

Raub, Patricia (1992). "Issues of Passion and Power in E. M. Hull's The Sheik." *Women's Studies* 21: 119–28.

Richey, Elinor (1980). "Kathleen Thompson Norris." In *Notable American Women: The Modern Period: A Biographical Dictionary*, edited by Barbara Sicherman and Carol Hurd Green, 509–11. Cambridge, MA: Belknap Press of Harvard University Press.

Riley, Glenda (1991). *Divorce: An American Tradition*. New York: Oxford.

_____ (1988). *The Female Frontier: A Comparative View of Women on the Prairie and the Plains*. Lawrence: University of Kansas.

Rosowski, Susan (1978). "Willa Cather's Pioneer Women: A Feminist Interpretation." In *Where the West Begins: Essays on Middle Border and Siouxland Writing*, edited by Arthur R. Huseboe and William Geyer, 135–42. Sioux Falls, SD: Center for Western Studies Press.

_____ (1981). "Willa Cather's Women." *Studies in American Fiction* 9 (Autumn): 261–75.

Rubin, Joan Shelley (1992). *The Making of Middle-Brow Culture*. Chapel Hill: University of North Carolina Press.

Ryan, Mary P. (1976). "The Projection of a New Womanhood: The Movie Moderns in the 1920's." In *Our American Sisters: Women in American Life and Thought*, edited by Jean E. Friedman and William G. Shade, 2nd edition, 366–84. Boston: Allyn & Bacon.

Scarf, Lois (1980). *To Work and To Wed: Female Employment, Feminism, and the Great Depression*. Westport, CT: Greenwood Press.

Schlissel, Lillian (1982). *Women's Diaries of the Westward Journey*. New York: Schocken Books.

Searles, Patricia and Janet Mickish (1984). " 'A Thoroughbred Girl': Images of Female Gender Role in Turn-of-the-Century Mass Media." *Women's Studies* 10: 261–81.

Stein, Allen F. (1984). *After the Vows Were Broken: Marriage in American Literary Realism*. Columbus: Ohio State University Press.

Strasser, Susan (1982). *Never Done: A History of American Housework*. New York: Pantheon.

Stuckey, W. J. (1966). *The Pulitzer Prize Novels: A Critical Backward Look*. Norman: University of Oklahoma Press.

Taylor, Helen (1989). *Scarlett's Women: Gone with the Wind and Its Female Fans*. New Brunswick, NJ: Rutgers University Press.

Thacker, Robert (1989). *The Great Prairie Fact and Literary Imagination*. Albuquerque: University of New Mexico.

Thiebaux, Marcelle (1979). "Faith Baldwin Cuthrell." In *American Women Writers: A Critical Reference Guide from Colonial Times to the Present*, edited by Lina Mainiero, 443–46. New York: Frederick Ungar.

Thurston, Carol (1987). *The Romance Revolution: Erotic Novels for Women and the Quest for a New Sexual Identity*. Urbana: University of Illinois.

Uffen, Ellen Serlen (1979). "Fannie Hurst." In *American Women Writers: A Critical Reference Guide from Colonial Times to the Present*, edited by Lina Mainiero, Vol. 2, 361–62. New York: Frederick Ungar.

Walker, Nancy (1988). *A Very Serious Thing: Women's Humor and American Culture*. Minneapolis: University of Minnesota.

Wandersee, Winifred D. (1981). *Women's Work and Family Values, 1920–1940*. Cambridge, MA: Harvard University Press.

Ware, Susan (1982). *Holding Their Own: American Women in the 1930s*. Boston: Twayne.

Weibel, Kathryn (1977). *Mirror Mirror: Images of Women Reflected in Popular Culture*. Garden City, NY: Anchor.

Wolff, Cynthia Griffin (1977). *A Feast of Words: The Triumph of Edith Wharton*. New York: Oxford University.

Woloch, Nancy (1984). *Women and the American Experience*. New York: Alfred A. Knopf.

Wood, Gerald (1983). "From The Clansman and Birth of a Nation to Gone with the Wind: The Loss of American Innocence." In *Recasting: Gone with the Wind in American Culture*, edited by Darden Asbury Pyron, 123–36. Miami: University Presses of Florida.

Index

About the Author

PATRICIA RAUB is currently Adjunct Professor at Providence College. She writes frequently on topics in American studies, popular culture, women's studies, and American history.